[RE] DO IT YOURSELF

ALSO BY JILL JARNOW

The Patchwork Point of View

[RE] DO IT YOURSELF

A Guide to Decoration and Renovation with Stencil, Folk Art Painting, Découpage, Collage, and Mosaic

Jill Jarnow

Drawings by the Author
Photographs by Herb Bleiweiss and the Author

THE DIAL PRESS/NEW YORK/1977

The Stenciled Kitchen Floor and the Stenciled Fruit
Cabinet on page 1 of the color insert appeared in the
Spring/Summer 1973 issue and in the Spring/Sum-
mer 1976 issue respectively of *American Home Crafts*
magazine.
Copyright © 1977 by Jill Jarnow

Library of Congress Cataloging in Publication Data

Jarnow, Jill.
  (Re)do it yourself.

  Bibliography: p. 171–172
  Includes index.
  1. Handicraft.   2. Decoration and ornament.
I. Title.
TT857.J37   745.5   76-882
ISBN 0-8037-1881-0
ISBN 0-8037-1882-9 pbk.

FOR ROSEMARY MACOMBER

Enthusiasm is contagious

ACKNOWLEDGMENTS

Many thanks to the people whose craft work has helped to make this book possible:

To Melanie and Michael Zwerling

To Betsy Potter

To Henriette Rattner

To Claudia and Sarah Gladstone

To all of the unidentified craftspeople whose work has been shown

Special thanks to Herb Bleiweiss, Rachel Newman, and Betsy Jablow
for their color photography, to Anne Knauerhase for her thoughtful
and constructive editing, and to my husband Al for his good
humor and ability to draw a straight line

CONTENTS

Contents

Introducing
(RE) DO IT YOURSELF

Welcome to *(Re)Do It Yourself* and to the pleasures of home improvement. If you are dissatisfied with your living environment, whether it be too rigidly arranged or too chaotic and jumbled, you can make significant, impressive improvements on a very small budget. Whether you are just beginning to set up your home or have been living in the same place for twenty years, *(Re)Do It Yourself* can help you. See how you can establish or improve the mood of your home with positive ideas and concrete action.

Learn to control and enjoy the way your home looks, and you will feel renewed excitement about the world outside. The trouble is, most people feel hopelessly overwhelmed by what they consider a cause already lost. But, as I hope to prove, it is never too late. In fact, the time could never be better. Redecorate some furniture or accessories that you already own, using techniques described in this book. You will give yourself a tremendous lift, and you will begin to give your home new style.

There are many practical as well as aesthetic reasons why you should consider redecorating (or even furnishing) your home with things that you already own or can find easily. New furniture, of course, is outrageously expensive. But aside from cost, the charm and craftsmanship of yesterday's factory-made furniture is quickly disappearing. Today's moderately priced wooden furniture is often partially made of fiberboard and masonite. Whimsical carving, graceful hardware, and pleasant proportions are being replaced by garish trims, plastic drawer pulls, and overbearing shapes. Fortunately, a great deal of our grandparents' furniture is sitting forgotten in basements, attics, and junk shops. You can often find it abandoned on the street—or undiscovered in your own living room.

ABOUT THE TECHNIQUES

If you glance through this book, you will see that there are many different crafts described for decorating and renovating your home. You will find stencil, the technique of decorating a surface by applying paint through a cut-out pattern; folk art painting, the direct method of decorating with brush strokes; découpage, the technique of cutting a picture from its background, arranging it on a hard surface, and sealing it in with many layers of varnish; fabric collage, the method of decorating with fabric and fabric trims; and mosaic, the technique of covering a surface by inlaying materials like tile, shells, stone, or other decorative elements. Each technique is explained in its own chapter, which contains an overall description of the craft, an in-brief rundown, suggested materials and applications and, finally, step-by-step projects. The projects themselves are arranged most often in the order that I myself did them or learned about them. Throughout the book, I have tried to be as honest as possible about the degree of difficulty of each project, although happily, all the skill that was required could usually be achieved with a little practice. I have tried to note potential difficulties as well as procedures that should go smoothly, the drawbacks of a technique as well as the strong points. I have also included several chapters on selection and use of materials as well as hints, both technical and aesthetic, that, hopefully, will add to your enjoyment of (Re) Do It Yourself.

To get started, consider the specific project suggestions. Decide how they apply to your individual needs and tastes, then get to work. Once you are familiar with color, style, and technique, you will be able to create your own wonderful furniture that will surpass anything made today. That's what (Re)Do It Yourself is all about—a new way of life and a new state of mind.

RULES, OR,
LEARNING THE HARD WAY

I like doing things that are easy and un-complicated. If a project sounds like too much trouble, I usually won't bother to try. On the other hand, if I really want to learn a new technique, but the rules sound too hard, I'll try to modify them for my own comfort. Sometimes I succeed, sometimes I don't.

My most dramatic success so far has been my Stenciled Kitchen Floor (page 88). I knew for a long time that I wanted to decorate the floor, but everything I read and everyone I spoke to (friends as well as salespeople) told me I had to use oil-base paint with polyurethane sealer for perma-nence. This had me stopped for a while. I couldn't get excited about working with materials that were slow to dry and hard to clean up. Eventually I hit upon the idea of using latex paint (which is water soluble and fast drying) for the decorative work and acrylic gloss varnish (which dries in 2 to 4 hours, instead of the usual 12) for the sealer. It simplified the process tremen-dously, and it also cut down on the aggra-vation. At one point I actually knocked over a can of paint, but because it was latex, it was no trouble to clean up!

On the other hand, every article I read about découpage warned me not to use old varnish. But I just happened to have a small can that had been lying around the apartment for a few years. Needless to say, the results were discolored and streaky. I learned the hard way.

My aim in writing (Re)Do It Yourself is to tell you about easy decorative techniques that you might never before have consid-ered. If you have even a touch of a decora-tive instinct (and you must, if you have read this far), I'm sure that you will be pleased with the processes as well as the results. I have recorded my experiences with the techniques to help you get started, being careful to let you know what worked for me and what didn't. But my approaches are not the last word on how something should be done (need there be a "last word"?). I don't, however, recommend breaking the rules too many times because you can't be bothered to follow the sug-gested plan. Certain classics, like keeping your brushes clean and allowing varnish to dry thoroughly between coats, are hard to improve on. Ignoring such recommen-dations usually ends up in frustration and, sadly, loss of interest. But if you feel that there is an easier way to do something, and that you have a reasonable chance of suc-cess, give it a try. I'll be delighted to hear about your conquest.

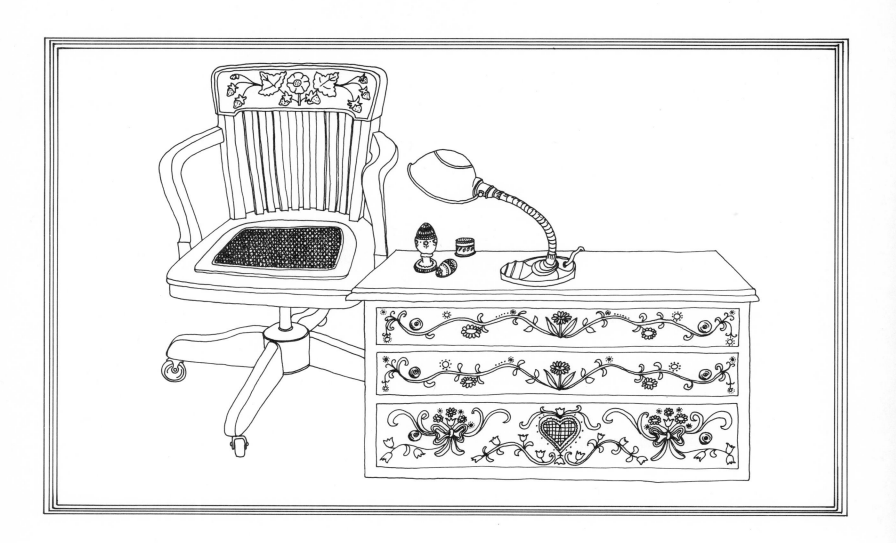

I
CONCEPTS

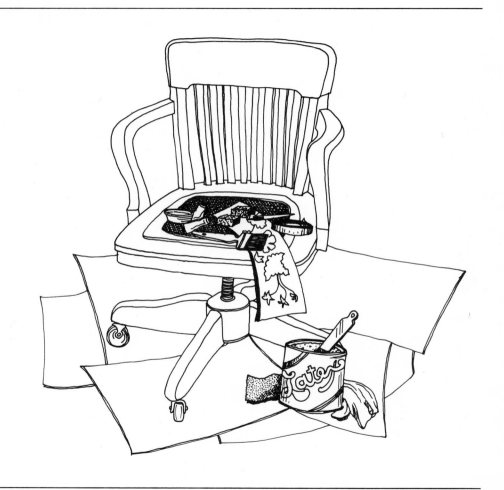

1
THE SECRETS OF SUCCESS

Perhaps you feel that you want to do something about the furniture and the decoration in your home, but you are afraid to begin. Although you are intrigued by some of the projects in this book, you have never done anything like them before. They seem as though they could be hard. Well, take it from me—nothing in this book is very difficult. In fact, most of it is easy!

Once upon a time not so long ago, I had never painted a cabinet, stenciled a chair, or even decorated a cookie tin. When I was in school I had worked on some isolated projects like stencil pictures and bean collages—and I loved doing them. But I hadn't thought about those things since then. Suddenly, I realized that whenever I could find an excuse, I was decorating some small object around the house—and I loved doing it. The enthusiastic reactions of my friends and relatives gave me courage. Soon I was doing bigger, more adventurous things like stenciling floors and painting mirrors. I was becoming so brave that I was able to tackle techniques like découpage and folk art painting that I had once felt were beyond me. Of course I made several mistakes, but at the same time I had many successes. Even now, I am still refining those crafts I am familiar with while experimenting with new ones. It's very exciting and gratifying. I plan to continue in new directions, and I hope my example will be an inspiration to you. From a person once afraid to paint a flower on a cookie tin, I am now one in constant search of something new to decorate.

Gaining self-confidence and acquiring design sense were for me the two biggest hurdles. They probably will be for you too. If you, like me, remember doing—and loving—small decorative projects when you were a child but have been afraid to get seriously "involved" with crafts as an adult, or if you are already proficient in one technique but are hesitant to learn a new one—help is here. I present to you a list of suggestions to help you develop the right skills and get into a positive frame of mind. But remember, self-confidence and design sense develop gradually, so give yourself a fair chance.

Included in this list are concepts that are important to me as a learning craftsperson. They are ideas that I often have to stop and remind myself of as I am working. Although this list is intended to apply to the crafts in this book, it includes concepts that are equally valid for other types of crafts or even other types of activities. They are also ideas that many established craftspeople won't "admit to." After all, what expert likes to admit to having once been inexperienced?

START SLOWLY

Begin on a small piece of furniture or an accessory. Try working on something you own that you consider a "lost cause." This way you can only improve it. I felt that way about my battered but comfortable desk chair. I am now pleased to refer to it as my Strawberry Desk Chair. It's on page 94.

GIVE YOURSELF A CHANCE

Once you have a few small successes, you will be more adventurous. In fact, you will be ready to tackle that depressing wooden dresser in your bedroom.

BE REALISTIC

You are not going to be able to transform a Victorian side table into a Louis XIV commode (but there are books on historic restoration if you are interested). On the other hand, you do have many viable, exciting choices. You will be able to change bleak, impersonal furniture into pieces that are warm, vibrant, and a joy to live with. If you long for traditional American shapes, look for reasonably priced reproductions in unpainted furniture stores. More contemporary pieces are also available as unpainted furniture. But shop very carefully because, alas, even unpainted wooden furniture isn't what it used to be. Better yet, choose from a variety of pieces in your local junk shop or charity organization or from something you already own. Chances are, you will choose something with great potential for decoration.

LEARN TO BE A GOOD DESIGNER— DO RESEARCH

Good designers aren't born, they develop. They are people who spend a lot of time browsing in libraries, bookstores, museums, and boutiques. They are people who have learned to know and appreciate what other good designers have done and are doing. So, if you want to develop your own talents, acquaint yourself with history, and stay up-to-date by keeping your eyes open and by saving magazine photographs, pamphlets, and newspaper articles. These clippings can be an invaluable source of inspiration to you in the years to come, so make sure to carefully file them away. Allow yourself to soak up outside influences, and don't be afraid to borrow a motif or color combination from something you admire. But make that interpretation distinctly your own. That's what good design is all about.

If you have been afraid to get started, I hope these hints have been helpful. Most often, friends see my crafts and are inspired to do their own. But occasionally someone will say that it looks too hard to do. I try to explain that I didn't just "magically" know what to do. I spent hours looking at pictures, reading in books, and browsing in shops. I tell about the failures that are hidden in the closet and the time I spent experimenting and learning. They don't realize that working with crafts is an ongoing process, that in order to improve my work I must learn from my failures as well as my successes. But I try to share with them the feeling of excitement and satisfaction. Mostly, I tell them that if they are really interested, they can do it too.

If you look carefully at almost any folk art design, you will soon realize that it is symmetrical. One side of the picture is the mirror image of the other. This simple form of organization is what saves much folk art from becoming visually chaotic. Instead, symmetry gives folk art charm and impact.

Knowing how to use symmetry is the key to producing well-balanced folk art designs. Especially if you have always professed that you can't draw, you will soon be able to create the most delightful motifs. All you need is visualizing paper (#620, available in art supply stores) or tracing paper (see page 51) and a sharp pencil. For help in keeping your lines and spacing even, put graph paper under the visualizing paper. If you feel more comfortable with pictures for reference (and who doesn't?), use something shown in this book, something in a source listed in the back, or anything else that you like.

Tracing is half the secret. The other half is knowing what to do with what you have traced. That's where symmetry comes in.

2
SYMMETRY: THE KEY TO FOLK ART DESIGNS

Use Symmetry to Form a Basic Shape

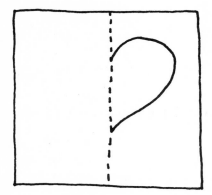

Draw half a heart shape on a piece of paper.

Fold the paper in half and trace it through.

Open the paper.

HOW TO MAKE A SYMMETRICAL DRAWING

Draw only half the shape. Fold the paper over exactly on the edge of the drawing and trace through the other half. A heart is a perfect example. Practice drawing them as shown and soon you will be a pro. To draw a flower, trace the heart onto a piece of layout paper. Fold the paper in half beneath the heart as shown. Trace the heart so that when you open the paper, you will have mirror images. Trace a third heart perpendicular to the first two. Fold the paper in half in the opposite direction from the first fold. Trace the heart through. Open up the paper and you will have a four-petalled flower.

SPECIAL NOTE: With all this folding and tracing, the drawings are sometimes on different sides of the paper. (Once you get started, you will know what I mean.) This is no problem at all if you are using visualizing or tracing paper. Just trace through whatever is on the back so that everything is on the same side. This will give you better visibility for working.

For a more elaborate motif, draw or trace a cluster of shapes. Fold the paper in half

HOW TO MAKE A SYMMETRICAL FLOWER

1. Trace the heart onto layout or tracing paper.
2. Fold the paper in half.
3. Trace the heart through and open paper.
4. Trace a third heart perpendicular to the first two.
5. Fold the paper in half in the opposite direction.
6. Trace the heart through and open paper.

1. Trace a cluster of shapes.

2. Fold the paper in half and trace.

3. Open the paper.

HOW TO DRAW AN ELABORATE MOTIF

and trace them through. Open up the paper and you will have a symmetrical design in the folk art style. If you aren't completely satisfied with the design, put a fresh piece of paper over what you have done and rearrange by tracing. Again, work on only half of the design.

If you have a specific area to decorate in mind, like the back of a chair or the top of a box, trace the outline of the actual surface to be decorated on a piece of layout paper. If necessary, piece the paper together with tape to get the correct size. If you can't see the outline of the shape through the paper (if you have taped the paper on top of the chair), work with sunlight or a lamp behind the object. To begin your design, fold the traced outline in half and work on one side.

Needless to say, it sometimes takes two or three tries to come up with a design that you like. You may have to put clean paper over what you have done and trace through only what you are happy with. Or put your efforts aside and begin again from scratch.

Use Symmetry to Form a Repeating Pattern

Draw or trace a simple motif. Cut a strip of layout paper and fold it into several equal sections as shown. Fold the first section in half. Center your motif using the fold as your guide, and trace. From this, trace the motif through onto all the other sections.

You can be as elaborate or as simple as you like when you use this method. Once you have tried it, you should never be intimidated by your drawing skills (or professed lack of them) again. You'll soon see that it's not drawing, but selection and arrangement that count. Use this technique to design for stenciling as well as decorative painting.

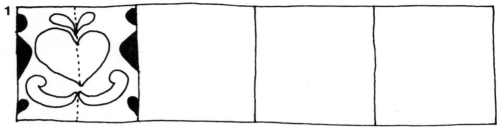

HOW TO MAKE A REPEATING PATTERN

1. Fold a piece of paper into equal parts. Center a motif in one section.
2. Trace the motif into all of the other sections.
3. Open the paper.

If you are interested in crafts now, chances are good that you enjoyed working on craft projects as a child. I know I did. In fact, many of the projects in this book are more developed versions of decorating I did when I was young. I remember painting on shells, gluing pebbles on bottles, and making doily collages. Whether with a school or scouting group, at home with friends and family, or off by myself, I loved dreaming up new craft projects—and then doing them.

I have included pictures of children's crafts here to suggest that many projects in this book can easily be adapted for children's use. Aside from the fun it can be for the child, it can also be very rewarding for you, as a craftsperson, to see the results. Children can be surprisingly inventive. I learned this from working with Claudia and Sarah Gladstone (ages 8 and 6). Once their interest was aroused in a project, they tackled it in a way all their own. The mosaic piece on page 5 of the color insert was done by Claudia, who was inspired by my mosaic work (as I had been inspired by the Grant's Tomb Mosaic). It was very excit-

3
CHILDREN AND CRAFTS

ing to see how she took a direction and further developed it in her own style. Her sister Sarah painstakingly collected, arranged, and glued down purple shell fragments on a carefully selected weathered board. The results were elegant.

Children at the beach often get involved in the traditional summer craft—shell painting. When I passed them on the walk one summer afternoon in Ocean Beach, New York, I saw myself twenty years ago. The shells and the enthusiasm of the children remain the same; only the tools have changed. Where I used to use cumbersome watercolors, these artists used felt-tipped markers! I was delighted to see that not only were the shells *decorated,* but that some were also painted with the message "Shells for Sale," lest there be any doubt of their business intentions—a very sophisticated advertising device.

If you are going to encourage children to start projects, make yourself available for consultation. I remember all too well the frustration of leaving a project incomplete because I didn't have the experience or the endurance to work out a technical snag. Help from a knowledgeable adult on choosing the right glue or paint or even some gentle advice on caring for materials might have made a big difference.

My husband Al and I live in an apartment furnished almost entirely with street finds, junk-store purchases, and family castoffs. Although we are badly overcrowded (we both work at home), we still can't resist examining a pile of furniture left on the street for the garbage collector. (You never know what treasures you might miss otherwise). Actually, we have "acquired" some of our favorite furniture that way. Many of our other pieces were rescued from family attics and basements. Still others were purchased at reasonable prices from used-furniture emporiums and antique stores. If you have never "shopped" this way, it may seem overwhelming or even haphazard. But the secret to good collecting is discrimination, imagination, and energy—and (of course) luck.

DISCRIMINATE!

A piece of furniture that is poorly made or beyond repair is worth passing up. Confronted with a piece that is severely caked with paint, consider carefully: Is it worth the hard work of stripping? See page 25.

4
LOST AND FOUND SHOPPING: MYSTERIES REVEALED

Bring into your home only what you can use. Furniture with no purpose will end up as clutter.

BE IMAGINATIVE!

Seek out objects that have good lines or pretty shapes. When considering a piece of furniture, look beyond the depressing veneer. Try to imagine it stripped down to pale wood, painted white, or cheerfully decorated. Sharpen your vision by looking at historic decorated furniture in museums, books, and magazines. Study the projects in this book.

If you are madly in love with a piece of furniture or see tremendous potential beauty in it, but have no obvious use for it, think hard. Invent your own uses. I keep sheets and towels in the bottom of the China Closet (page 22) (which, by the way, was a street find).

BE ENERGETIC!

Spend time researching color and design. Pick up paint swatches from your local paint store to see what colors you like in your home. Clip and file any magazine or newspaper pictures that might be an inspiration to you later, even if they don't seem to have any immediate use. Assemble materials and practice the techniques. Develop your skills, and when you are ready, put your energy into transforming your new finds into treasured pieces of furniture.

LUCK

So, keep your eyes open, happy hunting, and good luck!

One of my earliest experiences with (Re) Do It Yourself centered around the China Closet that now sits in the dining area of our apartment. Al, finding it ready for the garbage collector on the block where we live, dragged it home one day. It was dingy brown wood with the glass broken from the breakfront. He put it in the corner of his studio to hold art supplies, where it sat for several months getting encrusted with paint, turpentine, and dust. One day I could stand it no longer. I liberated it.

I had always thought that painting over wood was a sacrilege, but covering this depressing monster could only be an improvement. Out came the white paint (much to Al's horror) and soon we had a sparkling new cabinet. Actually, once it was covered with a few coats of white and began to show its potential, even Al got inspired. He added pale yellow paint to the trim and the inside shelves. He also added chicken-wire mesh (painted white, of course) to the breakfront door. As a final touch I lined the shelves with glazed paper. The China Closet has stood proudly in the corner of our dining area for several years,

5
DISCOVERING HOW TO (RE)DO IT YOURSELF

holding teacups and linens. Last year we gave it a fresh coat of paint. The art supplies have been moved to a new chest, as you shall see. Our China Closet is a cheerful, useful piece of furniture that constantly reminds me of the pleasures of (Re)Do It Yourself.

CHINA CLOSET

The projects in this book are meant to inspire you. The objects I chose to decorate and the patterns and colors I used are all appropriate to my home. I have included projects by other people that were inspiring to me. Hopefully, most of my needs and ideas will be classic enough to overlap with yours. But if this overlapping isn't exact—if you don't happen to have an old office chair or doll bed in need of decoration—please remember that *every technique I used can be applied to anything you might own.*

COPING WITH INSPIRATION

You are bound to have many inspirations. Inspirations are a very exciting part of the creative process. But beyond the first flicker of the idea comes the planning and the execution. Choose projects that you feel you can finish. If you get to the point in your work where you are unsatisfied or baffled, think it out or look for help. You may have to do more research or reevaluate your original idea. These project "standstills" are bound to happen. But persist. Don't let un-

6
PERSONAL VISION

finished projects sit around too long cluttering up your environment. Instead, let dissatisfaction with a project lead you into areas you might never before have considered. You will be infinitely more satisfied knowing you have worked a problem through to an inventive, pleasing solution.

THE BIG INVESTMENT

Before beginning your own decorating work, think carefully about what you would like to change and what kind of an atmosphere is realistic for you. Decide how much you have to invest. Be assured, however, that the major outlay need not be in dollars. Instead it should be in time, energy, and imagination.

Before deciding what to do to your potential treasure, consider your options. Part of the challenge of (Re)Doing It Yourself is to choose materials, techniques, and colors that are appropriate to your needs and tastes. You have three basic choices: you can strip a piece of furniture to bare wood and refinish it; you can cover an object with a solid color of paint; or you can decorate.

7
THE OPTIONS

STRIPPING

Stripping wooden furniture is hard, risky business. I once spent hours working on an ornate Victorian stool only to find that the wood underneath was ugly. I ended up painting the whole thing white, and it looks terrific. On the other hand, Al and I stripped years of varnish and dust from a roll-top desk and were delighted to find it was mahogany and curly maple underneath.

Many of our friends crave wood and will do almost anything to reveal the wooden surface of an article. A lot of beautiful old furniture does look wonderful stripped. For these pieces the work is justified. However, to assume that everything looks better in natural wood is a mistake. Too much heavy wood in a room can be oppressive and boring. I prefer to mix wooden pieces with those that are cheerfully decorated.

Paint and varnish stripper is available in hardware stores. If you have a yard and a hose, water-soluble stripper is great. Brush it onto the surface you are stripping as directed on the can and then wash away the residue with the hose. But watch out for glue in the joints. It will dissolve.

If you are working indoors, make sure the room is well ventilated, because the fumes are overpowering. Also be sure to wear gloves and have a large supply of newspapers and rags. Read all the directions on the label.

If your piece of furniture is covered merely with layers of shellac or lacquer, it can be stripped with wood alcohol.

There are professional furniture strippers who will remove layers of paint by soaking your furniture in a vat of lye. Although I have never had anything stripped this way, the concept sounds perfectly reasonable. To find the stripping service nearest you, check the phone book under Furniture Repair or Refinishing. Before surrendering your object, ask to see an example of finished work in a wood similar to your piece so that you will know what to expect. I have been told that lye baths are fine for softwoods and oak but are murder on hardwoods like mahogany. For more information on removing and replacing old finishes, read George Grotz, *The Furniture Doctor* (Doubleday).

Stripped furniture may be finished with wood stain, varnish, or furniture oil. It's always a good idea to test your intended finish in a place that won't show before covering the whole piece. Especially if you have spent days stripping something, spend a few extra hours to test the finish. Not only should you rub in a little stain or oil on a hidden spot, but you should also give it a few hours to soak in. I spent time, energy, and money stripping the hardwood floor in my first apartment. I bought an "oak" stain for refinishing it because it looked nice on the color chart in the hardware store. Having applied it to the floor with vigor, I stepped back to admire my work only to be horrified. The swatch in the store had been misleading. I had stained the floor a ghastly orange!

Just in case you suspect I am anti-stripping, I'm not. I have stripped a lot of furniture and have usually been delighted with the results. On the other hand, for most pieces of furniture, I find paint and decoration much more gratifying and personal. Once you realize the possibilities, I'm sure you will too.

PAINTING

Painting can be just the medicine for a depressing piece of furniture. Choose from a rainbow of latex colors available in your local paint store. If you give your project proper attention before applying paint, you will be well rewarded. Proper attention means removing all of the dirt, wax, or varnish that may have accumulated. Thorough removal usually requires a careful sponging—soap and water for dirt; alcohol for shellac; ammonia for wax—and a light sanding.

Expect to give an object three coats of paint. The first coat should be very thin. It won't cover much and you may be discouraged. The second coat will cover a little more, but the surface will still be slightly streaky. The third should cover completely. Always sand lightly between coats once the paint is dry to keep brush stroke marks to a minimum. Sometimes you can get away with two coats of paint, but often it takes a few more. Occasionally the old finish, if not thoroughly removed, will persist in bleeding through the paint. If so, let the paint dry and sand it down. Brush on liquid gesso (available in art supply and hardware

stores) to seal the old finish. Once dry, sand the surface lightly and begin applying paint again. Anything that continues to bleed through the acrylic gesso can be covered with a layer of varnish, sanded when dry, and then painted. Wait for the gesso to dry thoroughly before applying the varnish.

I do all of my indoor painting with latex paint. It goes on easily, dries quickly, and is easy to clean up before it is dry with soap and water. It comes in a wonderful range of colors in flat, semi-gloss, and enamel finishes. If you want your finished object to be

shiny and can't find the color you want in latex enamel, use flat latex and varnish over the finished piece.

Whenever possible, buy a good quality paint. Good paint is worth the extra money because it will cover an old surface faster (therefore you'll use less), will go on smoother, and will last longer. If you use cheap paint and get splotchy results, you'll be dissatisfied.

Applying paint to a badly encrusted surface is only a stopgap measure. As you will see, it will begin to peel off in a few weeks. If a piece is covered with layers of paint and is no special prize, leave it in the attic. If you are determined to use it or suspect that it is a valuable antique, read the section on stripping furniture. Naturally, it's easiest to work on an old wooden piece that can be merely washed and sanded down. Glance through this book and see if you recognize any of the silhouettes. Most of the furniture, before being painted, was dark Victorian or undistinguished office furniture. For information on paint, varnish, and brushes, turn to page 35.

PAINTING WITH WHITE

White furniture is very satisfying to live with because it gives a special elegance to even the most downtrodden environment. Al and I have painted many things in our apartment white—from dressers to dining-room bentwood chairs (discarded by a candy store!). In my work area the book-shelves are white, as are the supply boxes. It probably sounds as if we live in a snowy white apartment. We don't. But there is so much color in our papers, books, and supplies that the touches of white furniture give visual order to potential chaos.

I have even begun to convert my friends to the joys of white paint. One woman, who was about to move into a new apartment wondered what she could do to make her new home special. After a lot of thought, she took a deep breath and painted her piano white. The transformation was so pleasing that she also painted her dining room table and chairs white!

Victorian and other types of ornate furniture, easily found in junk shops, lend themselves particularly well to white paint. The original finish is dark and depressing. Both Victorian furniture, decorated with whimsical carvings, and later, Art Deco pieces, decorated with geometrics, are enlivened by white paint. We have a white Victorian console table in our tiny entry way. Aside from the visual cheer that it brings to the corner, the white paint also makes the area seem larger.

If you are still skeptical about using white, try an experiment. Choose something dark and ornate, like a picture frame or a side table. Wash and sand it and then give it a few coats of white paint. If it's a picture frame, hang it up. If it's a table, put it in a dark corner. I'm sure that the area will immediately look more cheerful and that you will find yourself painting more furniture white.

DECORATING

If you are interested in the challenge of decorating your furniture and accessories, you have an entire world of possibilities to consider. You can stencil a design, paint a pattern, découpage a picture, or collage a texture. For information on each technique, read the appropriate section later in this book. There are several considerations to work out.

Practicality

You may have a collection of seashells and a chair that needs redecoration, but it would be uncomfortable to sit on a chair covered with shells. Save the chair for a more appropriate technique and hunt up an old box or pot or mirror to cover with shells.

Placement

The technique, the design, and the color you choose to decorate with should be geared to blend with the future surroundings of the finished object. Although a brightly colored cabinet might look out of place in a dark, sophisticated den, a découpage accessory would probably look fine. Most likely you would want to keep to bright colors if you are painting furniture for a child's room. Of course, all this is hypothetical advice because I can't possibly know what your decor and tastes are. But my suggestions are meant to help you make intelligent decisions so that your new creation will have a place in your home. In most cases, hand-decorated furniture is flexible enough to fit in gracefully with the most sophisticated or most primitive surroundings.

Economy

Do you want to paint a cookie tin with a paint that costs $15 a half gallon? Some of the colors that I used for the Stenciled Fruit Cabinet on page 1 of the color insert cost that much. The paint store would not mix colors in less than half gallons, but since it was the only way to get the colors I wanted I splurged. I had a lot left over, so eventually I mixed it into softer colors for the Strawberry Desk Chair on page 94, the Shell Stencil Chair on page 96, and the Découpage Table on page 127. If you too can make your paint go far, by all means use custom-mixed colors. If not, choose good quality pre-mixed paint or mix your own as described on page 39. Why pay extra for the luxury of custom-blended paint if you aren't going to use most of it?

ENGLISH
PEPPERMINT
LOZENGES

8
COLLECTIONS

If you enjoy decorating your environment, you should be a collector. Small objects grouped together on a shelf, mantel, or tabletop add life and charm to a room. Collections need not be made of priceless antiques. Instead (and probably more fun) they can be composed of things like eggs and eggcups, decorative boxes, or even seashells. The only requirement is that you love looking at everything on display. Anything that you grow tired of should be stored away. My own egg and eggcup collection grows rapidly. Not only do I add to it, but friends, feeling my enthusiasm, contribute to it when they want to give me a gift. I also enjoy adding to their collections.

Collect items with intriguing patterns or colors that will inspire you as you decorate your environment. An enticing teacup that you discover in a thrift shop should be placed where you can enjoy it. Perhaps its colors or pattern will influence you when you choose paints or designs for a project.

If you really want to be prepared to deal with your decorative whims, save articles like empty wooden spools, cookie tins, and pieces of fabric. Always keep a small supply

**DECORATING
WITH YOUR COLLECTION**

of cans, jars (with lids), rags, and boxes on hand rather than disposing of them. When you are on the beach, collect shells and pebbles. In the woods, collect leaves. Soon you will see that it is not the idea of the finished product that comes first, but the challenge of exciting materials.

But watch out not to become bogged down by your collections (I bet you were wondering when I'd get to that). The trick is to keep your materials beautifully arranged. They should be either neatly stored away or carefully displayed so that you feel completely in control of them.

When a stack of magazines becomes oppressive, look through it. Extract any articles or pictures that you might want to save. Those of special importance should be tacked up on a wall or bulletin board; the rest should be stored away for easy reference. Some magazines have interesting advertisements as well as articles. These should be left intact.

Buttons, beads, and shells stored in glass jars are cheerful enough to keep in view. Decorating supplies like paint and glue are best stored in drawers or on an inconspicuous shelf. Other materials may be stored in shoe boxes, milk crates, or straw baskets. If the boxes and crates are to remain in the open, take time to decorate their surfaces, and potential chaos can turn into unexpected inspiration. To me, it is worth going out of my way to make my studio environment pleasurable because working there is what I like to do best.

II
MATERIALS

LATEX

Water-base paints were used on every project in this book that was painted or stenciled. Latex paint, meant for use on walls, works equally well on chairs, tables, and floors. It comes in a terrific range of colors and finishes, is durable, a pleasure to apply, and easy to clean up when still wet with soap and water. For more on latex paint, turn to page 27. Acrylic paint, discussed later in this chapter for use in decorative work, is also water base.

Choosing Colors

Choose colors carefully. Don't just ponder over the charts in the store. Bring home sample swatches (which every manufacturer provides) and see how they look in your own environment. After all, how many people live with the same fluorescent lighting found in most stores? If someone had suggested this to me several years ago I would have ignored it, thinking the suggestion "a fussy detail." But once you try it,

9
PAINT

you'll see what I mean. Paint swatches look completely different at home.

Paint also looks different when it's wet in the can or on your brush from when it's thoroughly dry. This may be a problem if you are mixing colors yourself. Invariably the paint will dry a shade or two off from what you thought you had. Consider painting a small test swatch. Let it dry completely before applying paint to the final surface. You can only learn to predict these color changes by experience and even then, the color can still be a surprise.

Hints for Using Latex Paint

Open cans with a screwdriver, butter knife, or the rounded end of a can opener.

Always ask for extra wooden paint sticks for stirring paint when you buy paint. Sometimes you won't get them, but you can re-use the ones you have—both ends if necessary. Once the paint is thoroughly dry on the paint stick it won't run into the other colors.

Here's a tip I read in a book. It really works! When a can of paint is freshly opened, hammer holes with a nail around the inner rim of the can so the paint that usually accumulates and cakes there can drip back into the can. You will then be able to close the can tightly after each use. Sometimes it helps to hammer the lid on using a rag as a cushion between the lid and the hammer.

Save old cans of white latex paint for mixing and storing pastel colors. Otherwise use a coffee can with a plastic lid or any other recyclable container with a cover.

Wash all of your brushes in lukewarm water and mild soap immediately after use. When still wet, latex and acrylic (discussed below) paints wash out easily, leaving the brush spotless. When dried and caked with latex or acrylic paints, brushes can only be cleaned with a special solvent.

Use latex right from the can, or, if you are really fastidious, pour it first into a clean container or paper paint bucket.

ACRYLIC PAINT

Artists' acrylic paint comes in small, expensive tubes or jars and is available at an art supply store. Use it for small amounts of special colors or for decorative work. Choose latex house paint to cover an entire surface and add the decorative trim with artists' acrylic. Latex wall paint and artists' acrylic are both water-soluble plastic paints and can be intermixed (with discretion). I do it all the time. But be practical. If you have a large can of latex white and need to make it light blue, squeeze in a small amount of blue acrylic. Stir well. But don't squeeze a pound tube of acrylic white into a drop of latex blue. That's wasteful! By the way, try not to mix a gallon of light blue if you need only a pint, although sometimes it can't be helped. I have mixed colors by adding "a little of this and that." I got my color eventually, but I had mixed five times as much as I needed. For more on economy, turn to page 29.

Hints for Using Artists' Acrylic

Use artists' acrylic by squeezing a small amount onto a palette, which can be any nonporous surface such as an old plate, a sheet of glass, a tin can, or palette paper (available in art supply stores). A plastic egg tray from the five-and-ten is the most fun, though, because when the paint is thoroughly dry, you can easily peel it out, leaving the surface fresh and clean.

Never, under any condition, combine water-soluble paint (acrylic and latex) with oil-base paints. Oil and water don't mix.

Polymer Medium

Polymer medium is an acrylic, water-soluble artists' medium available in art supply stores. Mix small amounts of polymer with acrylic colors to make the paint easier to handle. Polymer medium is available in matte and gloss finishes. The matte will allow the paint to dry flat, while the gloss will add some shine. I use and recommend mixing gloss medium with acrylics for painting and stenciling designs on a gloss or semi-gloss surface. That way, when the decorative work is dry, the project is complete (except for the addition of antiquing if you choose).

Polymer medium should be thinned with water. If, however, your brushes dry with medium or acrylics—or both—in them, you will need special acrylic solvent (available in art supply stores) to get them clean. But don't let wet brushes sit around when it's so easy to wash them in a glass or under running water.

MIXING COLORS

Today latex and acrylic paints are available in such a wide range of colors that you should be able to find just what you want by looking at color charts and swatches. Be sure to read page 37 for special hints on selecting colors this way.

Sometimes, however, you may want to mix your own colors. Perhaps you have a lot of paint left over from a previous project. With a little practice you should be able to mix some of it into new colors.

That's what I did with paint left over from the Stenciled Fruit Cabinet on page 85. Or you may need such a tiny amount of color that it seems silly to buy a whole tube or can. Of course, you might want the pleasure and extra freedom of knowing that you can blend just what you want at home.

Mixing paint, a skill to be respected, can be learned with experience and common sense. Think back to the basics that you learned in elementary school. There are three primary colors that cannot be mixed from anything else. These are red, blue, and yellow. Combined, in various amounts, with white or black, they will give you almost any hue.

Remember:
Yellow and Blue make green
Red and Blue make purple
Red and Yellow make orange

Mix the three primary colors together and you will get brown. Add white to any of these colors and you will get a pastel. Add a tiny amount of black and you will make the color darker, but add too much and you will make mud. With these basic rules you will be able to make many colors.

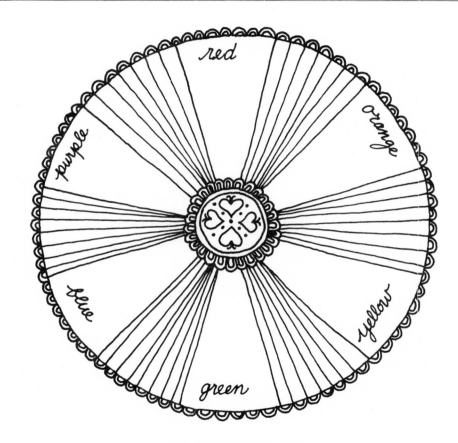

THE COLOR WHEEL

Here is a little more information that can make a big difference in color mixing. Look at the color wheel. The colors that oppose each other on the wheel are called *complementary colors*. They are:

Red and Green
Yellow and Purple
Blue and Orange

Add a tiny bit of green to red (its complement) and you will mix a deeper, more mellow red. Add a tiny dot of purple to yellow, and you will get a rich, yellow ochre. Add orange to blue, and you will have a grayed blue. To make a richer, more interesting color than what you have in the tube, add a tiny bit of that color's complement. But add drops at a time, because when complementary colors are mixed together in equal parts, they make brown.

Using complementary colors as a basic color scheme when decorating can be very striking. The Stenciled Fruit Cabinet is basically red and green.

Special Note on Mixing Acrylic Pastels

Acrylic paints, which I have recommended for all decorative work, have a tendency to become chalky and lose their vibrancy when mixed with a lot of white. Being a real fan of pastel colors, I discovered that there are several ways to overcome this problem.

1. As often as you can, buy good quality acrylic paints. These probably will contain more pigment than the bargain variety and therefore will stand up better to the addition of white.
2. Add white to your acrylic color slowly and mix thoroughly before adding more.
3. If you find yourself constantly mixing pastel colors that become chalky, consider investing in containers of Cel Vinyl, manufactured by Cartoon Colour Company. This is the paint used by animation artists for making cartoons and is used the same way as acrylic paints. Available in a few art supply stores such as Art Brown in Manhattan, it can also be ordered directly from the Cartoon Colour Company, 9374 Culver Boulevard, Culver City, California 90320.

Although a small container is considerably more expensive than an equivalent-sized tube of acrylic, the Cel Vinyl colors go further, retain their vibrancy, and can be intermixed with acrylics. By the way, there's no need to pay extra for the Cartoon Colour white. Acrylic white from the local art supply store is fine.

Varnish is a clear plastic, turpentine-soluble liquid that is brushed on a surface to provide a tough cover resistant to water, heat, alcohol, and chemicals. In the past, varnish was made of hard-to-handle natural resins. But modern, synthetic resins are easy to use and give a more durable finish.

Varnish is easy to apply. Just brush it on a clean surface and let it dry thoroughly. Sand lightly with extra-fine sandpaper, dust carefully, and apply a second coat. If the varnish seems too thick and leaves brush strokes, add up to 50 percent turpentine until the varnish goes on smoothly. To thin out varnish you have already applied, brush it over with a small amount of turpentine until it is smooth. Experts never dip their brush directly into the can, but instead pour the varnish into a clean container before beginning to work.

To remove tiny air bubbles that form as you work, gently dust the tip of your brush (which should be as dry as possible) over the surface when you have finished all the varnishing.

10
VARNISH

Keep the object you have coated out of direct sunlight for the first few minutes that it is drying to avoid the risk of bubbling. Whenever possible, I put a freshly coated project under a lamp—but not too close.

Unfortunately, varnish is slow to dry and therefore collects dust. If you apply the varnish in a reasonably dust-free room, allow each coat to dry thoroughly, and sand lightly between coats, you should have no trouble.

Varnish only on dry days, because when the air is damp, it will take the varnish longer to dry, giving your project more opportunity to collect dust.

TYPES

Varnish is available in satin, gloss, and all-purpose crystal clear. Buy it in hardware and paint stores. The drying time varies from 4 to 12 hours, as described on the label. The satin finish usually takes the full 12 hours to dry, while the gloss is usually more quick-drying. In each project description I mention what type of varnish I used

(if any). Follow this as a guide if you are new at varnishing, or read the labels, look at the color charts, and experiment. Naturally everyone prefers a quick-drying varnish, but these usually have a high shine. Although this tough, glossy surface is excellent for stenciled floors, satin-finish varnish, which is more delicate, is better for découpage.

Buy whatever varnish you like but make sure it is meant for indoor use. Avoid outdoor or spar varnish (unless, of course, your project will be placed outside).

Buy varnish in small quantities because as it ages it turns colors, causing streaks. Unfortunately, I learned this the hard way. If you are doing a large project like a floor or a wall, of course it's wise to buy in larger amounts.

Quick-Dry Découpage Varnish

I have also experimented with quick-dry découpage varnish, which is available in hobby shops. Although it has a plastic base, it is *not* water soluble. It requires a special thinner, available where you buy the var-

nish. True to its name, it dries in 20 minutes (or the kind I have does). But there are certain drawbacks. It's hard to handle, and if you mix in too much thinner, it will dissolve the acrylic-base paint on the object you are coating (disaster!).

ANTIQUING OR GLAZING

Sometimes when a découpage, stencil, or folk art painted project is finished, it looks "too perfect" and "too new." By adding antiquing or glaze, you will add a special touch of dignity to your finished piece, making it easier for it to blend in with its surroundings.

Antiquing is essentially adding "dirt" to a decorated surface in an artistic way. Although there are many commercial antiquing kits available, you will save money and get more satisfaction from your work if you buy separate ingredients and make your own antiquing glaze. It's really very easy. Mix equal parts of turpentine, linseed oil, and raw or burnt umber oil color (from a tube). If you have saved any tin cans or jars, use one for mixing your glaze. For a large piece of furniture, you will need to mix about a cup. For smaller projects, mix less. You will also need a stiff brush for applying the antiquing (buy an inexpensive one at a hardware store), cheesecloth or rags for wiping it away, and plenty of newspapers to protect everything in the general vicinity. Antique solution is oil base (unlike the acrylic water-base paint you probably used to do the decorative work) and it tends to fly around, so make sure everything is well covered before you begin to work. You may even want to wear rubber gloves, although it isn't necessary.

When you are sure that your decorated piece is thoroughly dry, you may begin to antique. Do not sand it before you begin or the antiquing won't look right. If you are working on a piece that has drawers, remove them and work on them separately.

Apply the glaze solution directly to the surface of the project with a stiff brush. Although you can actually scrub the glaze on with careless abandon, work with some restraint lest you spatter yourself and everything else with specks of brown.

When the piece is entirely covered, including the cracks, the crevices, and the design, begin to wipe away the antiquing with a soft cloth. Work gently, in a circular motion, trying to imagine where the piece would be dirtiest if it were really old. These areas should be left covered with a little more glaze.

Learning when to stop rubbing takes experience. Some people prefer to leave a lot of "dirt" on the surface of their project, although I prefer the way pieces look almost completely wiped down. The antiquing, though not too obvious, leaves just the finishing touch I like. It's always better to rub too much away and then add more, but if you find that you have left too much on the piece, it can be removed with mineral spirits. The important thing is that no matter how much glaze you leave, you must avoid making fingerprints that can detract from the beauty of your finish. If the piece you are working on is to get heavy wear, you may want to give it an extra coat of varnish, but make sure the antiquing is thoroughly dry first. It takes about 24 hours.

Antiquing With Acrylics

Quickie projects, or those that can be completed in an hour or two with quick-dry découpage varnish, may be antiqued with equal parts of polymer medium and acrylic raw or burnt umber, though you really have to work fast. In fact, if you are working on a large area, antique small sections at a time so that the glaze doesn't dry before you can wipe it away. If your glaze has been sitting for only a few minutes, you can remove most of it by wiping it away with a wet sponge. Don't use acrylic brush cleaner to remove unwanted glaze or you will remove the decorative work underneath too. Rub each area with a soft cloth as with oil-base glaze.

Acrylic antiquing *should not* be considered a substitute for traditional oil-base glaze. It doesn't have the same luster, delicacy, or controllability. I use it mostly on découpage projects that I have completed with quick-dry varnish (see page 44).

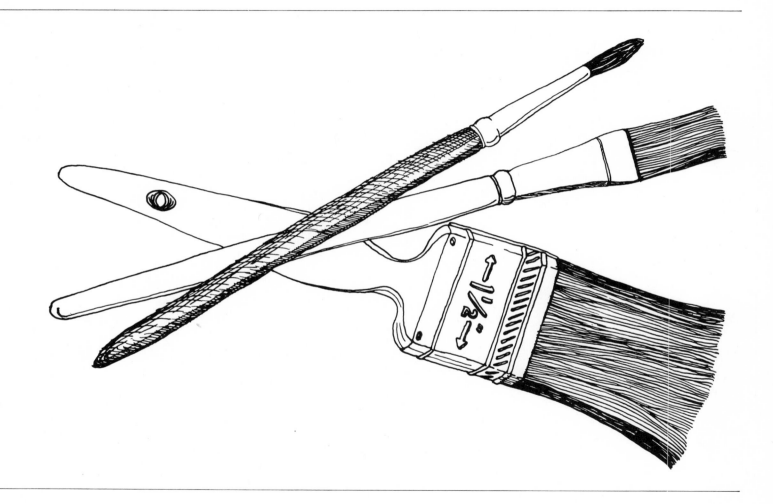

FOR SOLID-COLOR AREAS

For painting a solid color on a wall or a piece of furniture with latex paint, use a flat, medium-priced brush from a paint or hardware store. Try to make a reasonable judgment about size when choosing a brush for a specific job. A brush that is too big will be unwieldy when painting the arms of a chair. A small brush will make unnecessary streaks and take twice the time to cover a large floor.

I also recommend using a small, soft, good-quality ½-inch flat brush from an art supply store for coating small areas like ornate trim and objects like trinket boxes.

Once you have two or three brushes to choose from, you should be able to handle just about any job.

FOR DECORATIVE WORK

You'll be shocked when you go to an art supply store to buy a small, round good-quality brush for decorative painting. They are expensive, especially when you compare them in price to the larger, synthetic

11
BRUSHES

brushes meant for flat painting. But a good-quality brush is a wise investment. If it is natural sable, it will perform well for you and last a long time—if you take good care of it. I use a number six brush for all decorative work.

SPECIAL CARE

Never leave a good brush sitting in a glass of water for more than a few minutes. You will destroy the point, which was what the big investment was all about. Instead, swish it around in a clean glass of water until all the paint is out. Run the ferrule (the metal part that holds the bristles) and the bristles through a rag or paper towel from the handle of the brush down to shape the bristles into a point as shown on page 101. Then lay the brush down. If you have finished using the brush for the day, wash it more carefully in lukewarm (never hot!) running water and mild soap. When you are sure that all the paint and soap are out, dry as described above. Always store a brush on its side or with the bristles up in the air.

SPECIAL NOTE: Sometimes new brushes have hardener in the point to make them look fancy in the store. Don't press down on the bristles while the hardener is still in them. You'll ruin the brush. Instead hold the brush under cool running water until the hardener is dissolved. The point will suddenly seem twice as big as the one you thought you bought. If you follow the method suggested for drying the bristles, you will be able to bring the point back down to the original size.

CARE OF VARNISH BRUSHES

Varnish is oil base so you must use turpentine or turpentine-base brush cleaner for washing brushes that have been used for varnishing. Pour the turpentine (or brush cleaner) into a can or jar and soak the bristles of the brush in it for a few minutes. Sometimes it helps to swish the bristles around in the liquid and tamp them against the sides of the container. Remove the brush and wipe down the bristles with a clean, dry rag. If the brush is still dirty, immerse it for a few more minutes, and repeat the process. When you are satisfied that the brush is clean, rinse it with mild soap under cool water.

Most of the materials needed for the crafts in this book are available in an art supply store or a hardware store. Specialty items like boxes to découpage can be bought in hobby or craft shops that are springing up all over the country. Mosaic tiles, available in these hobby shops, can also be purchased from tile distributors. I have always found the phone book enlightening and time-saving when looking for materials, so check the listings in your area. Also, be inventive. If your local hobby shop doesn't carry unpainted accessories for découpage, check the housewares section of the hardware store. When buying supplies don't limit yourself to what the manufacturer describes on the label of a can. You can stencil or paint furniture and accessories with latex paint meant for use on walls.

12
BUYING MATERIALS

SOME SPECIAL ADDRESSES

Here is a list of shopping sources in the New York area and a few listings for mail-order houses around the country.

Brandon Memorabilia, Inc.
1 West 30 Street
Room 202
New York, N.Y. 10001
Carries prints and reprints great
for découpage.

Adventures in Crafts
218 East 81 Street
New York, N.Y. 10028
Carries everything for découpage, plus materials that can be used for other crafts,
including an assortment of glazes, wooden
boxes, and containers. A catalogue is not
available at this writing.

Arthur Brown and Bro., Inc.
2 West 46 Street
New York, N.Y. 10017
Calls itself the world's largest art supply
store. If your local art shop doesn't have an
item, check here. A catalogue is available.

Azuma Stores
415 Fifth Ave.
New York, N.Y. 10016
If you live in New York, of course, there
may be an Azuma store nearer you than
this one. Check the Manhattan directory.
If you don't live in or visit New York, this
is the branch that handles mail orders.
They carry a selection of reasonably priced
seashells by the bag, as well as beads and
just about every other inexpensive item for
the home. No catalogue is available at this
writing. Check similar Oriental import
and gift shops in your area.

LeeWards
840 North State Street
Elgin, Illinois 60120
Has a mail-order catalogue of craft and
sewing supplies that boggles the mind.
There are over twenty branch stores,
so check to see if there is one near you.
P.S. Pay attention to the supplies—not
the kits!

Buy paints, brushes, and varnish in your
local hardware store, art supply store, or
hobby shop but beware of packages designated specifically for craft use. Once a
product has this label, the price will be artificially inflated. Of course, if you find a
box to decorate or a jar of a special color
paint that you can't resist, the cost is understandable. But with the exception of a few
special products, don't assume that because
a package is marked "antiquing kit" (for instance) it is the only thing you can use. It's
surprisingly easy, not to say economical, to
mix your own antiquing (see page 44). In
addition, it's much more satisfying to develop enough independence to look beyond
the prepackaged products that threaten to
dominate our lives.

CONTACT PAPER AND DECALS

Aside from your local art supply store, hobby shop, and the special suppliers listed on page 49, hardware stores and five-and-ten-cent stores are full of potential decorative trims. Among these are decals, stickers, and contact paper. Choose decals that depict charming fruit and flower motifs. Ignore grotesque animals and heavy-handed still lifes. Some contact paper is patterned with traditional ginghams and florals that can be used beautifully. Avoid poorly styled damasks, wood grains, and modern designs.

Use decals and contact paper for quicky projects. I have perked up spice jars with bouquets of Victorian flower decals, or a cluster of dime store stickers. I used contact paper to cover the Summer Bar on page 144. But don't let your decorative efforts stop with these materials. If you have the decorative instinct, experiment with other materials and techniques. They may take more time and thought, but the results are proportionately more attractive and gratifying.

PAPER FOR DESIGN WORK

Tracing paper can be found in most stationery stores or five-and-tens, but if you are near an art supply shop, invest in a pad of layout or visualizing paper (number 610 or 620) instead. Almost as translucent as tracing paper, it's more durable, easier to use, and so much more pleasant to the touch that you'll never buy tracing paper again. For hints on how to design in the folk art style using layout paper, turn to the section on Symmetry on page 11.

GLUE—WHAT KIND TO USE

All lightweight gluing in this book—on the Pasta and Grain Containers (page 153), the Shell Flower Pot (page 162), and the découpage projects, for example—was done with white glue from the five-and-ten-cent store. Projects to receive heavy wear, such as the Mosaic Floor (page 155) and the Pebble Sink (page 160), were done with tile adhesive from the hardware store or tile supplier.

Fabrics (the Fabric Collage Clothes Rack on page 139) were glued in place with spray adhesive from the art supply store. Trimmings were affixed with white glue. When buying spray adhesive, be sure to read the label carefully first to make sure the product is suitable for your needs. Then follow the directions on the can. Be sure to work in a well-ventilated room because the fumes are overpowering. Cover everything surrounding the object being sprayed with a generous amount of newspaper, because the adhesive is hard to remove and can cause real problems if it lands on an unintended surface.

III
TECHNIQUES AND PROJECTS

POINTERS FOR SUCCESS

All the techniques in this book are easy!
Here are some secrets for succeeding with
them.

Preparation

Decide on your design and assemble the
materials before you begin work. Make sure
the object to be decorated has been properly cleaned or prepared (see page 27). For
specific information on each technique,
read the appropriate section.

Patience

Be sure each step is complete. For example, when stenciling, wait for the paint
to dry before applying the next layer of
color so you don't smudge what you have
done. Fortunately, if you use latex paint,
you won't have to wait very long. When
working with découpage, make sure each
layer of varnish is bone dry before applying
the next, or you will end up with a
gummy mess.

13
INTRODUCING
THE TECHNIQUES

Respect the Tools and Materials

Close cans of paint, varnish, and glue tightly when you are finished working so they don't dry out prematurely. Wash brushes used for acrylic paints and medium thoroughly with cool water between coats of paint, so that they are always in top condition and ready for use. If your brushes are damaged or caked with paint you will not be able to control your brush strokes. Wash varnish brushes in turpentine or brush cleaner and then rinse in cool soapy water.

Practice

Acquaint yourself with any of the techniques that are new to you before you tackle a project. Work on a scrap of wood or cardboard for experience. Do a preliminary small project before you commit yourself to a large one. Once you are confident that you can control a technique and cope with any small problems that may come up, you will be able to concentrate on design.

Relax

Use these techniques to make happy, thoughtful, useful changes in your home.

COMBINING STENCIL, DÉCOUPAGE, AND FOLK ART PAINTING

Just because the three techniques—stencil, découpage, and folk art painting—are discussed in different sections in this book, it doesn't mean that each must be used exclusively by itself. When used in combination, they can produce striking results. In fact, many of the projects in this book are a combination of techniques. The Stenciled Chairs (pages 94 and 97) are decorated with delicate touches of brushwork that would have been difficult with stencil. The Découpage Trinket Box (page 133) is trimmed with a painted line around the outside edge of the découpage artwork for a more complete look.

ENLARGING A DRAWING

Method 1—Mechanically

When you see a motif or pattern in a book or magazine that you want to use for a decorating project, you will have to enlarge or reduce it to the right size. The easiest way to enlarge an image, and the way craft books never mention, is to have the artwork photostated. Look in the phone book for the photostat service nearest you.

Artwork to be photostated should be drawn or traced in dark black ink on white paper. Decide how much of an enlargement you want and mark it clearly below the picture. The information should be presented with the extremes of the drawing marked with the new size. Remember, you will not be able to change the proportions by enlarging (or reducing) artwork. If you mark the 4-inch side of a 3- by 4-inch drawing to be enlarged to 12 inches, the 3-inch side will automatically become 9 inches.

Order a positive, matte-finish photostat, which is the less expensive variety. Don't be put off by the spots and the unimpressive finish of the matte stat, because all that's necessary is that you can see the lines clearly. If you are having something enlarged beyond 16 by 20 inches, the stat may have to be "pieced." This, too, is perfectly all right for your purposes.

Some large photostat houses give same-day service. Others will need longer to complete the work.

If you are a student or work in a school that has an opaque projector, you're in luck. Ask someone to show you how to use it. Tape a piece of paper on the wall or screen and trace your enlarged artwork.

ENLARGING A DRAWING MECHANICALLY

enlarge to 12" / pos. matte stat

Method 2—By Hand

You can also enlarge a drawing at home without any mechanical aids.

Trace your drawing onto layout (see page 51) or graph paper (tape the graph paper over the drawing on a window for greater clarity). Using a ruler, mark off equal squares right over your drawing, as shown. Next place a much larger sheet of layout paper over your drawing and draw in the top and left-hand side borders of the drawing. Then, using your ruler, draw a diagonal line—begin at the upper left corner of the design and extend it beyond the lower right corner until you have reached the size you need for the enlargement. Fill in the lines to complete the new, larger rectangle.

Mark off the new rectangle with exactly the same number of squares as the first rectangle. Then make a dot in each spot where a line crosses the smaller grid in the same location on the larger grid. When all of the locations are marked, connect the dots. Your enlargement will be complete.

For information on transferring the artwork to the surface of your project, turn to page 106.

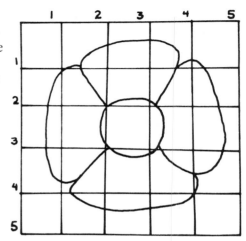

HOW TO ENLARGE A DRAWING

Trace your drawing onto layout paper or graph paper. Mark off equal squares right on top of the drawing.

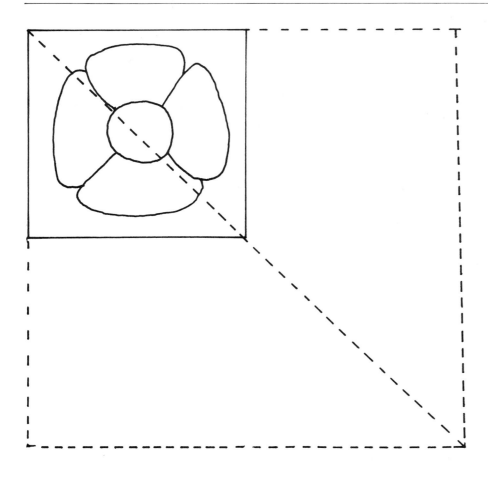

Place another sheet of layout paper over your drawing and draw in the top and lefthand side borders of the drawing. With a ruler, draw a diagonal line from the upper left corner of the design through and past the lower right corner until you reach the size you need for enlargement.

(Step 3 on next page)

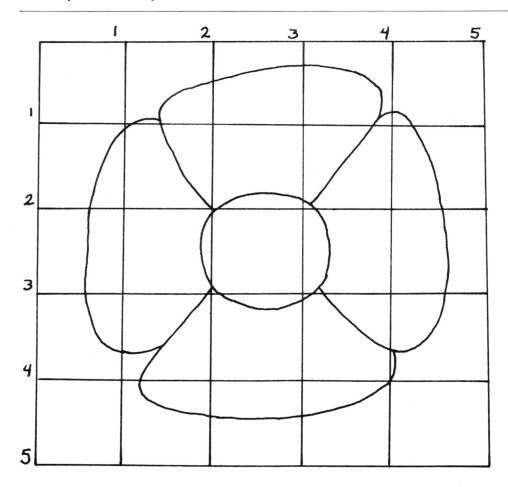

Fill in the lines to complete the box. Mark off the new box with exactly the same number of squares as the first grid. Make a dot on the larger grid in each spot corresponding to where a line crosses the smaller grid. Connect the dots.

IMPROVISATION—YOUR OWN SPECIAL TOUCH

In describing many of the projects in this book, I have presented the original plans I made for them and then the completed piece. Often there is a discrepancy. I find it more enjoyable if I allow myself freedom to make changes as I work. I like to allow for the possibility of artistic "accidents." These unexpected turns are what makes my work distinctly my own. I hope you will learn to feel this way about your own crafts. But don't confuse this relaxed attitude with sloppiness or bad workmanship, which can only detract from the appearance of a finished piece. Instead, think of improvisation in terms of changing your mind about the shape of a flower while you work, or making a sudden addition of an extra decorative border in your own personal style. Try to be as neat as possible in your work, but recognize that you, as a craftsperson, and the techniques you are working with, each have particular, unavoidable quirks.

WHERE TO WORK

If you have access to an attic, a basement, or an empty room, you're in luck. I haven't been so fortunate. My own workplace is meant for drawing, sewing, and small projects in general. Now that I'm working on larger pieces, I've had to be more inventive.

What to Do With a Large Piece of Furniture

If a piece of furniture that you already own is too large to move or if you have no place to move it to, paint it where it stands! Take out any drawers and prop them up on chairs. Painting a piece in position proves to be great incentive for getting the job done quickly, while it also prevents you from bringing pieces into your home that you have no place for.

Wherever possible, turn the object to be painted or varnished face up. This will prevent most drips. If there just isn't room, be prudent with the amount of paint or varnish that you take on your brush. An overloaded brush will cause annoying drip marks.

Work in a good light. There is nothing so unnerving to the craftsperson (that's you and me) as moving a finished project from the security of darkness to revealing sunlight.

Perhaps you will feel more confident in the beginning if you work at decorating a small accessory. There are probably many things around your house that could use some perking up—a cookie tin, an old juice jar, a basket. Accessories are a good place to start decorating because if you successfully cheer up a shelf or a countertop, you will soon expand your work to include corners and whole rooms. Besides, an accessory project with which you are dissatisfied is easy to remedy by painting over or (in the case of certain inevitable disasters) by hiding from view.

The next few pages contain some suggestions for accessories to decorate. More are listed on page 108. For information on a specific technique or project, check the table of contents and turn to the appropriate section.

14
DECORATING ACCESSORIES—A GOOD PLACE TO BEGIN

DECORATING TIN OR METAL

A decorated tin object like a watering can, planter, or canister can be a great gift or a terrific visual pick-me-up for your home.

The hard work—that of painting the object a solid color—is already done by the manufacturer; all you do is add your magic touch. Get out your acrylic paints, gloss medium (see page 39), and brush, and you're all set.

There is one necessary step you must take to keep the painting process easy and pleasurable. *Wash all metal surfaces down with vinegar.* You may dilute it with up to 50 percent water, but I have found that straight vinegar works best. The vinegar will etch the tin surface so it is porous enough to hold the paint. If you neglect this 5-minute preparation, each stroke of paint will vanish—in front of your eyes—into a million tiny beads. It's happened to me and it's frustrating. If the vinegar doesn't work and the paint won't stick to the surface, try lacquer thinner next. It's hard to tell exactly what mixture has to be used to seal the metal surface, and sometimes vinegar just isn't strong enough. Beyond these precautions, the rest is up to you.

Read the section on Decorative Painting in the Folk Art Style, which begins on page 99. Then transfer a design to the surface of the tin or paint a design freehand. Whatever you choose, Happy Birthday!

DECORATING NATURAL WOOD

Don't forget that you can decorate a wooden object without coating the entire thing with paint. Brighten a drab wooden chair by painting or stenciling a garland of flowers across the back. Wooden cheese boards, bowls, and spice containers can be trimmed with color to make beautiful, personal gifts. If you are an impatient craftsperson, or a last-minute shopper, decorating natural wood is for you because there is no waiting for three coats of a base color to dry. Paint directly on the wood with acrylics or latex. If you want a gloss in your finished work, mix in some polymer (page 39). For more on paint, see page 37.

DECORATING EGGS

Consider eggs when you are thinking about something to decorate. Because of their beautiful shape and hard surface, they make a great base for decorating. All of the techniques in this book—découpage, mosaic, stencil, and painting in the folk art style—are great to use.

First prepare the egg for decorating by washing the surface with mild soap and water. This will remove the natural oils that later might prevent the paint or glue from holding properly. Next you may blow the insides out of the egg: Prick a tiny hole at the top and bottom of the egg with a sharp needle or pin. Shake the egg gently in your hand first, to break up the yolk inside for easier removal. It will also be easier to remove the insides if the egg is at room temperature. Blow the contents of the egg gently (for both your sake and the egg's) into a bowl.

Decorated Eggs

1. Decoupage
2. Folk art painted
3. Pasta and grain mosaic
4. Bead mosaic

Blowing out an egg is slow and often frustrating work. It can be tedious and still result in disappointment if you accidentally drop the egg as you are blowing it out. Therefore I decorate eggs *without* removing the insides, which decreases my chances of dropping an egg before the decoration is complete! When I tell a friend who is admiring the decorated eggs on display in my apartment that they are intact, I am often met with a horrified stare. But the fact is, when an egg gets old, the insides harden up without causing any noticeable changes in the egg's surface. A broken egg in this dried-up condition is no more annoying to clean up than one that has been blown out.

Whichever you choose to decorate, the cleaned-out egg or the intact egg, remember, eggs are fragile. Egg decorators should be prepared to keep their efforts displayed well out of harm's way. Even then some breakage is unavoidable. Although you may be able to keep most of your creations indefinitely, be prepared to lose a few. But think positively. A broken egg is a good excuse to decorate another one.

DISPLAYING EGGS

If you enjoy decorating eggs, plan to display them in the style they deserve. Keep them in a small basket or a French egg rack (found in the housewares department of better hardware and department stores). Or decorate eggcups specifically for your eggs. Unpainted wooden eggcups, great for folk art designs, are available in houseware departments, as are solid color ceramic ones, great for mosaic.

EGGCUPS DECORATED WITH FOLK ART

PAINTING BASKETS

Perk up straw baskets from the five-and-ten with a few flicks of your paint brush. I decorated my first basket out of desperation when I couldn't find any cookie tins to decorate, and inadvertently stumbled on a whole new direction.

Paint with acrylics (page 39) right on the straw. Sometimes the paint soaks in, which makes a lovely, muted effect. Or you can keep the color more brilliant by coating the basket first with polymer medium (page 39). Let the medium dry and then apply paint.

Timid little marks get lost on the surface of woven baskets, so be bold. Use a broad, flat brush to put down areas of color. Let the structure of the basket suggest a pattern to you, or impose your own design right on the weave.

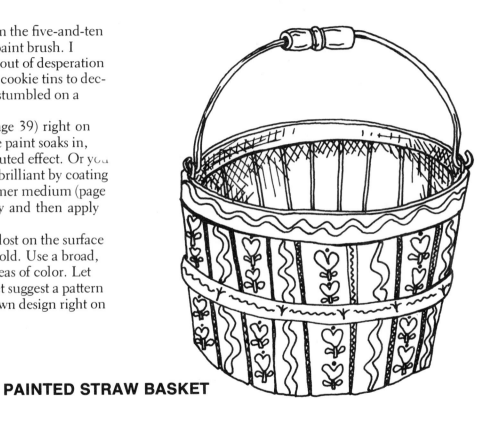

PAINTED STRAW BASKET

15
STENCIL

Stenciling is the technique of transferring a design to a surface by applying paint through a cut-out pattern. Although stenciling has been used for centuries by people of all cultures, it can be seen in its most striking usage on the decorated floors and walls found in Early American homes. The soft, powdery shapes and whimsical designs have been nearly forgotten, however, with the disappearance of the home-decorating craftsman and the advent of inexpensive, mass-produced wallpaper and flooring. Most people today are totally unaware of the beauty and practicality of stenciled decoration. But now that paints are so easy to use and the color selection so vast, I hope that if you are adventurous enough to take aesthetic control of your surroundings you will learn to love the technique of stenciling.

My first experience with stencil as a home decoration was several years ago when I decided to redecorate my dreary linoleum kitchen floor. Early in my plans I resolved to make the project as technically simple and as inexpensive as possible (without, of course, jeopardizing the visual effect). Having had a brief introduction to the technique in school, I decided on stencil. To get bright, clear colors and to avoid the problem of sticky, unwieldy materials, I chose to use latex paint, with varnish as a sealer after the decorative work was complete. The choice of materials was not easy. Every paint salesperson that I consulted looked at me askance and practically told me that I was wasting my time. I went ahead with my project anyway, determined that even if it had never been done before, there was no reason why I couldn't succeed.

I am delighted to report that I was right. Not only was the latex paint with varnish sealer a pleasure to apply, but I have been living with the Stenciled Floor for three years now and it is still glossy, clean, and satisfying to look at. It requires no waxing because I gave it six coats of crystal-clear floor varnish. Water with ammonia will usually remove most of the dirt that falls on it, and stubborn scuffs disappear with a few flicks of a plastic scrub pad. If the shine should get dangerously dull (and therefore

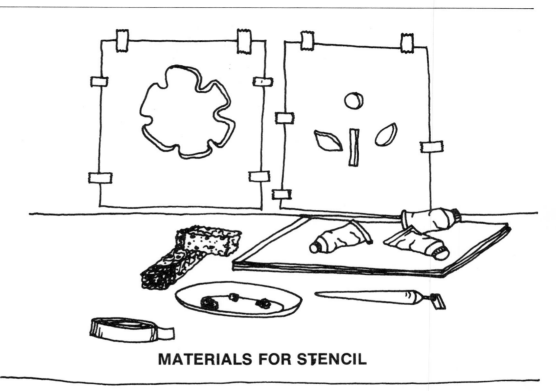

MATERIALS FOR STENCIL

stencil paper	layout pad	stencil knife
paint sponges	palette	masking tape

worn down), I would certainly consider giving the floor a few more coats of varnish, but this doesn't seem imminent.

If you are considering stencil as a decorative element in your home, let me encourage even the tiniest flicker of a thought. It is one of the simplest, prettiest, most gratifying of all the decorative techniques. Of course a large project, like a kitchen floor, may take almost a week to complete, but stencil decoration on chairs (see page 94) can take less than an hour, once the chairs are sanded and painted.

Although there is written material available on the traditional approaches to stenciling (see page 172), I have found that these techniques can be streamlined without sacrificing the charm or visual impact.

STENCIL-IN-BRIEF

1. Preparing the surface
2. Applying the base paint
3. Cutting the stencil
4. Applying the paint through the stencil
5. Varnishing or antiquing (optional)

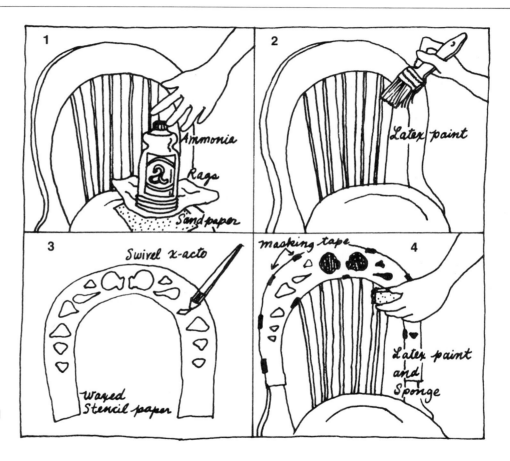

What to Choose to Stencil

Choose any flat surface for your stencil work—from the top of a cookie tin to the kitchen floor. Avoid curved surfaces for your first few projects because the stencil, when in place, will buckle slightly, making it difficult to apply the paint.

Preparing the Surface

Make sure that the surface you are decorating is clean, free of grease, wax, or dust, by rinsing it with a mild solution of ammonia and water. If you are stenciling on slippery enamel paint, sand lightly first. If you are stenciling an old piece of furniture, turn to page 27 for more information. For information on preparing a tin object, see page 104.

Choosing or Designing a Pattern

Choose a design from this book, from a book listed on pages 171–72, or from any other source. Or, better yet, devise your own. For information on designing with symmetry, see page 11.

Look carefully at the stencils presented here and in other sources to understand the limitations of the medium. If you want to stencil an elaborate design, you will have to convert your drawing into several stencil plates as shown in the illustrations on the following pages. Cut a separate stencil for each color you intend to apply, and then use the stencil that covers the largest area first, as shown. However, colors that are not near or do not overlap each other in your design can be included in the same stencil.

DESIGN FOR STENCILING

Applying the paint with a sponge

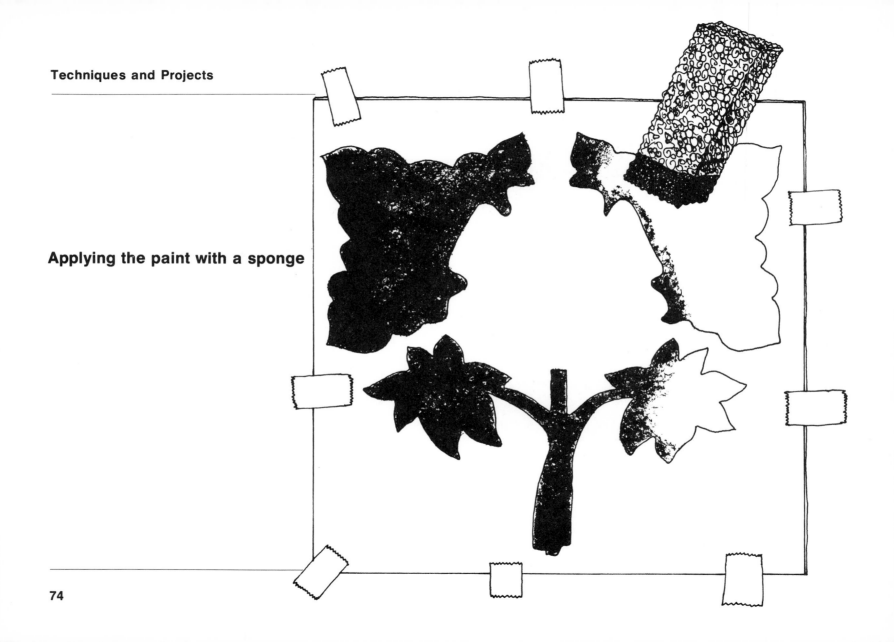

Plate one: the leaves

Plate two: the flower and leaf veins

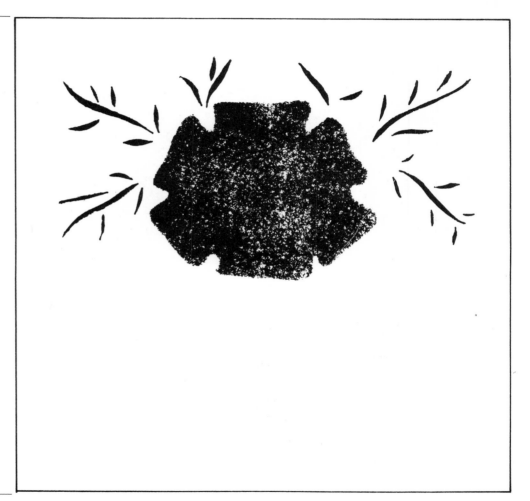

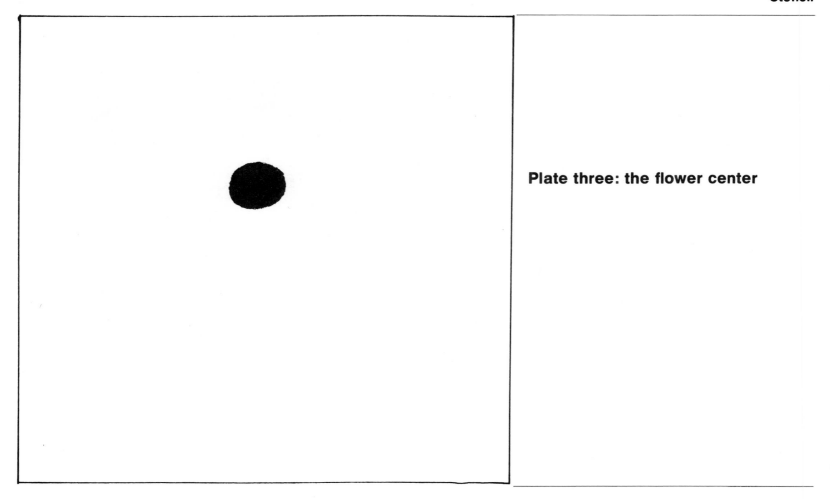

Plate three: the flower center

The Complete Stencil

Choosing Stencil Paper

There are two types of stencil paper generally available in art supply stores. One is a heavy, opaque, oiled board. The other is a translucent, heavy-duty waxed paper. I prefer the translucent type because it allows me to see what I am doing as I put the stencil in place. However, the opaque variety is more durable and is better if you are planning to use your stencils over and over. Since I try to use the translucent waxed paper whenever possible, all of the descriptions are given in terms of that paper. If you do use the opaque stencil paper, you can transfer your design to it by sandwiching carbon paper between it and your drawing.

Transferring a Design to Translucent Stencil Paper

Trace or design your drawing on layout paper (page 51). Tape your drawing to a tabletop with the stencil paper taped over that. With a hard pencil or, for a more visible line, a felt-tipped marker, trace the drawing through to the surface of the stencil paper. If you are using a pencil, press hard. If you are using a marker, be careful not to smear the lines with your hand.

Cutting the Stencil

Remove the drawing from underneath the stencil paper so you don't cut into it and re-tape the stencil securely to a cutting surface so it won't move around. Cut against heavy cardboard, inexpensive chipboard from the art supply store, or a pile of newspapers. You can even cut against the back of your layout pad if it is large enough.

The best tool for cutting your stencil is a small knife with a swivel blade from the hardware store or art supplier. Use it with the point against the paper, as shown. Regular X-acto knives or a single-edged razor blade will also work, but the swivel blade is more manageable on curves. The most important thing, whatever blade you choose, is that it be sharp. A clean edge is important when you apply paint to the stencil. The swivel blade, which is the most expensive of the three types I have suggested, lasts longer. The other two blades should be replaced frequently—as soon as they begin to lose their edge. When your knife needs more than a firm stroke to make a clean cut, it is time to change the blade.

If you work slowly cutting against cardboard or a pile of newspapers with a sharp blade, you should find stencil cutting a breeze. If you have any long, straight lines in your design, use a ruler to guide you as you cut.

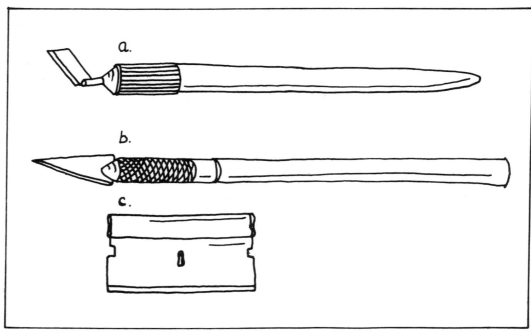

STENCIL CUTTING TOOLS

a. swivel blade knife
b. X-acto knife
c. single-edge razor blade

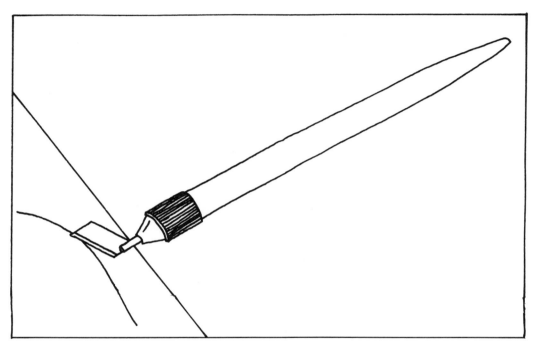

Cut the stencil with the tip and sharp edge of the blade.

Using Masking Tape

If you are decorating a large area like painting a rug on the floor, or you have planned many straight lines in your design, use masking tape as your stencil. Put down the tape where you want a stripe or straight line and then paint in the area with flat color, working right onto the tape. When the paint is thoroughly dry, peel off the tape. Then, if you want to remake a stripe, lay down tape on both sides of the stripe that was left unpainted and brush in paint between the two strips of tape as shown. You can also use tape, as I did on the Stenciled Fruit Cabinet (page 85), to make a pattern. I painted the background a solid color. When it was dry, I put down tape to form a diamond-patterned tablecloth. Then I painted over the entire area. When the paint was dry, I removed the tape and had a wonderful harlequin pattern. Later I drew lines within the stripes with a brush, freehand.

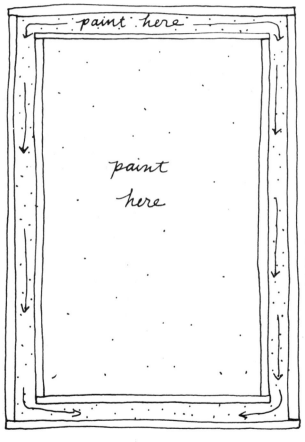

paint here

paint

here

USING MASKING TAPE FOR BORDER STRIPES

1.
Put down tape, paint, let dry.

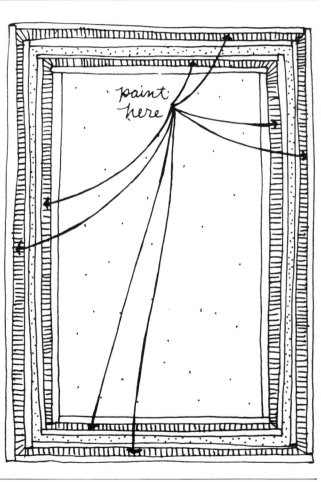

paint here

2.
Remove tape, put more tape on both sides of stripes left blank, paint, let dry, remove tape

Removing the Masking Tape

Waiting for the paint to dry thoroughly before removing the tape can be a true exercise in patience. Once the paint appears dry (5 to 10 minutes) the temptation to remove the tape is overwhelming. Sometimes you can get away with it, but more often than not, if the paint isn't thoroughly dry, you will remove paint as well as the tape. Sometimes (and this can really be discouraging) the paint will come off with the tape even after you are sure that you have waited long enough. There are, thankfully, a few solutions. Stop peeling! Then, with a fresh single-edged razor blade or X-acto knife, carefully cut along the edges of the tape with the blade. Let the edge of the tape guide you, but be sure to cut into the paint only—not into the tape. Press firmly and work slowly so your cuts will be as straight as possible. When you have gone over all of the outside edges of the tape, begin to remove the tape again, slowly. If, while you are peeling the tape away, you see that you missed an area with the blade or didn't cut deeply enough, stop peeling and cut again.

The second way to prevent paint from coming up with the tape is to sand the surface you are working on lightly before putting down the tape. This will give the paint something to grip. It may be too late to sand the piece you are working on at the moment, but it's a good thing to remember for the future.

Try to remove the tape as soon as the paint is dry. You may have difficulty removing tape that is left on for several hours.

Affixing the Stencil in Place

Tape the prepared stencil in position on the surface to be decorated with a few small pieces of masking tape so you won't have to worry about its shifting while you work.

What Kind of Paint

As with all the other projects in this book, water-base acrylics from the art supplier or latex from the hardware store are best to use. For more on these paints, turn to page 37. Remember that spray paint is *not* water-base paint.

What to Apply the Paint With

I am happiest applying paint to a stencil with an inexpensive sponge, which I cut into several manageable pieces, although a stiff stipple brush (from the art supply store) or a can of spray paint will also work well. If you use a brush, you have to worry about cleaning it after each color or you must buy several (and they are expensive). If you use spray paint, you have to contend with the paint's falling beyond the outer confines of the stencil.

How to Apply the Paint

Whatever tool you use, sponge, brush, or spray can, the secret of applying paint to a stencil is the same: it must be done with moderation. If you use a sponge or brush, make sure the paint is very dry on the tool. Dip the sponge into the paint and then wring the excess back into the container with your fingers. Then dab the sponge on newspaper to make sure it's really dry. Dip just the flat tip of the stipple brush into the paint and then "bounce" off the excess on a sheet of newspaper before applying the brush to the stencil. Any loose paint that you don't remove from the brush or sponge will run under the stencil and cause smudges. It is better to apply paint in several thin, controllable coats than in one heavy one.

If you are stenciling with spray paint, use the same caution. Read the directions on the label of the can and apply the paint in several thin layers. For even application, move the nozzle of the can along the surface of the stencil rather than turning your wrist and the can to reach a far corner. Be very careful not to hold the can too close to the surface you are spraying or the paint will drip.

When to Remove the Stencil

Once you have applied paint through the stencil, give the paint several minutes to dry before attempting to remove the stencil paper, or you will smear your work. If you are planning to apply your next color over what you have just done or close to it, give the paint 5 or 6 minutes to dry before you lay down your next stencil sheet. Fortunately, water-base acrylics and latex paints dry quickly, so you won't have long to wait.

Finishing Touches

When your stencil work is completed, you can touch up rough edges with a paint brush. If you have stenciled a large area like a wall or a piece of furniture, coat the finished product with satin, crystal-clear, or high-gloss varnish to protect your work. If you have stenciled a floor, give it at least three coats of varnish. My kitchen floor gets a lot of traffic, so I gave it six coats of quick-drying crystal-clear. The varnish dried in 3 to 6 hours, so I was able to put

down two coats a day. The extra time I took applying the protective varnish has paid off in the durability of the floor. For more on varnish, turn to page 43.

When Not to Varnish

If you are stenciling a small object like a box or a toy, mix a small amount of polymer medium (page 39) in with your acrylics. This will give the stencil work strength and a finished "glow." If you are stenciling with gloss or semi-gloss latex on a glossy surface, you can omit the polymer. But for objects that will be getting heavy use, like a tabletop or serving tray, varnish is still best because it is heat, moisture, and alchohol resistant.

THE STENCILED FRUIT CABINET

Al and I bought this cabinet from the Salvation Army to fulfill our growing demand for storage space. I was attracted to its white enamel top and whimsical square shape. Al liked its size and the convenient shelves already inside. With a fresh coat of white paint, it sat in my studio for months being very useful and looking very much like the forgotten cousin, tolerated only for its utility.

Eventually it occurred to me that this little storage cabinet had the potential to be exciting as well as useful. Studying photographs of decorated furniture, both antique and present-day, I decided that stenciled images and border stripes (made with the help of masking tape) would be most appropriate. Since the cabinet was really meant for the kitchen, it would be decorated with fruit. I let the shape of the door and the drawer suggest the design.

THE STENCILED FRUIT CABINET

I worked out a design on a sheet of graph paper, using pictures of traditional furniture for reference. When I felt I had a strong design, I traced the actual size of the drawer and door onto some layout paper (which I had to piece together to have a large enough sheet). I drew my design on this paper. You can find these master drawings on grids on pages 174 and 175. Next I traced the drawing onto translucent stencil paper in three stages. Stencil plate one was the bowl and some fruit, plate two was leaves and more fruit, and three was the highlights on the bowl and leaves. I used three separate stencils to be able to get a layered effect without running the risk of colors mixing into each other.

I began by taping off the door stripes—putting the tape where I didn't want paint—and brushing the color into the exposed areas with a ½-inch soft brush. Because it is better to put down a succession of thin coats rather than one heavy one, the first coat was very streaky and unattractive. It took all my concentration to allow the first coat to dry thoroughly so I could apply the next one. I also had to wait patiently for the paint to dry thoroughly before I could remove the tape. In fact, the temptation started to overcome me, and I was soon sorry. Since the paint wasn't completely dry, it started to come up as I pulled on the tape. (In fact, if the surface you are painting is less than spotless or is too slick—say, painted with high-gloss enamel—the paint will not adhere well.) From this experience I learned to run a single-edged razor blade along the edge of the tape to ensure that it will separate properly from the paint when removed. Of course, I felt I shouldn't be so fanatical that I couldn't allow for some imperfection. Part of the beauty of hand crafts is the human element.

When the stripes of color around the outside edge of the door were completed, I did a patterned tablecloth ground plan by placing tape in a crisscross pattern.

I cut the stencils out with a sharp swivel-blade knife, marked the front of each stencil plate with a big **F**, and taped the first one in position.

All of the work was done in latex paint, which made things easier.

To apply the paint, I used some inexpensive sponges cut to ladyfinger size (that way I could use both ends). I kept the sponge very dry so the paint wouldn't run under the edges of the stencil. Of course, a little running is sometimes unavoidable, so if you find that you have been too generous with your paint, and you have unquestionably smeary edges, you can always touch them up afterward with a paint brush.

The fruit and fruit bowl were applied in several layers of paint so they are opaque. I dabbed on a layer of paint, waited a few minutes for it to dry, and then dabbed on more. The highlighting, however, was done in just one dabbing. Once you begin to stencil, you will enjoy experimenting with texture and color density.

When all the stenciling was completely dry, I put on two coats of satin-finish varnish.

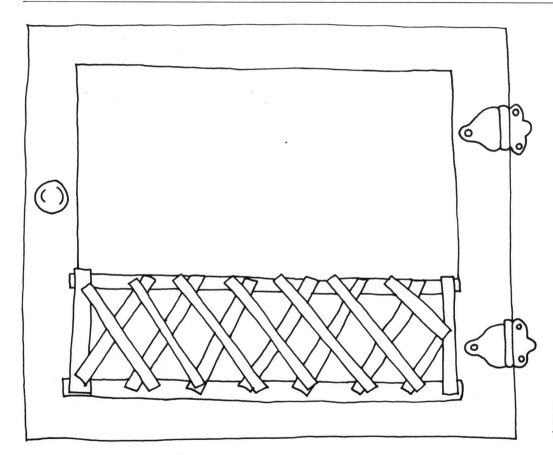

Laying down masking tape
in a crisscross pattern
to paint tablecloth

THE STENCILED KITCHEN FLOOR

My Stenciled Kitchen Floor (also mentioned on page 3) was a carefully thought-out solution to the "dreary kitchen floor blues." Looking at its cheerful colors today, it's hard to remember that underneath is depressing linoleum.

I planned the design of rabbits, hearts, flowers, and turtles using symmetry with the aid of graph paper according to the method described on page 11. All the designs were drawn on layout paper and cut from translucent stencil paper. Before beginning the decorative work, I washed the floor thoroughly with ammonia and water to remove any old wax. When it was dry, I gave it a light sanding and wiped it clean. With a yardstick and pencil, I marked out my plan right on the floor. This meant drawing in all of the straight-line borders and the central medallion. Next I taped off as many of the straight lines as I could with masking tape. I used 1-inch and 1½-inch masking tape to mark off all the border stripes and the central medallion outline. Then I painted the color between the tape with a small, flat brush, being sure

**THE
STENCILED
KITCHEN
FLOOR**

to keep the paint from lapping over the outer edges of the tape. The lines I taped were separated by an area of color so there was room for the tape. I gave all of these masked-off areas two coats of latex paint, allowing the paint to dry thoroughly between coats. When the second coat was completely dry, I slowly removed the tape. Then I masked off more areas with tape and painted them in. Since the floor had been properly cleaned and sanded before I started the decorative work, there was no problem removing the tape. If you, however, find that you have trouble removing tape, turn to page 86 for some help.

When all the flat areas of color in the design were painted in, I taped off the outside edge of the pattern and the surrounding walls and painted the remaining linoleum (outside the design) a flat color.

SPECIAL NOTE: To prevent any scratching or scraping to the latex paint, I removed my shoes and worked in my socks. The soft surface of the socks is even more desirable than bare feet, which tend to leave marks. Once one coat of protective varnish was down, I didn't have to be so careful.

When the floor was completely covered

STENCIL DESIGN FOR KITCHEN FLOOR
(Opposite and Above)

with areas of solid color paint, I was ready to begin stenciling. The stencils had been prepared according to the instructions on page 79. I did the stencil work with latex paint and sponges as described in that section. I worked from the inside section out toward the edges, applying the central flower motif first, the rabbits, flowers, and turtles next, and then the repeating border designs.

It took me about three days to do all the stenciling. When it was complete and thoroughly dry, I applied several thin coats of high-gloss varnish, as described on page 44. The whole job, from start to finish, took about six days. There's no doubt that it was inconvenient to have the kitchen inoperable for that time, but we managed to work around it, and the results were well worth waiting for.

My Stenciled Kitchen Floor appeared in *American Home Crafts* magazine in the Spring/Summer 1973 issue. The photograph shown here was taken in the spring of 1975 and the floor still looks new!

For more on stenciled floors, read about Melanie's Stenciled Dining Room Floor, which follows.

**STENCIL DESIGN
FOR
DINING ROOM
FLOOR**

THE STENCILED DINING ROOM FLOOR

When my good friends Melanie and Michael Zwerling moved into their new apartment, Melanie was determined to have an elegant dining room. Knowing that the room she had in mind measured 6 feet by 12 feet, I wondered how she would do it. Michael, I have since learned, was equally curious. The solution lay in Melanie's imagination, energy, and careful control of dramatic elements. In a room that could be mistaken for a closet, Melanie stenciled a rug on the floor, painted the walls deep-eggplant purple, and created a fantastic Shell Mirror (see page 164). She painted the woodwork white, hung eyelet curtains, and kept everything else simple and light.

The hardwood floor had been freshly sanded, so Melanie worked directly on it, marking off the borders with masking tape. She made sure that the paint was completely dry and the surface was not too slick, so that the tape would not pull up the paint when it was removed. (If you have this problem, turn to page 83). When the

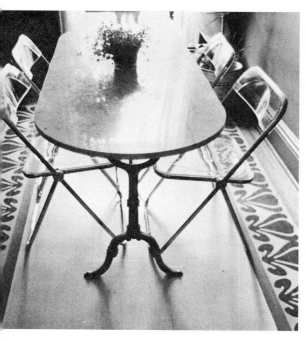

DETAIL OF FLOOR

THE STENCILED
DINING ROOM FLOOR

solid areas and stripes were completed, and the tape removed, Melanie was ready to stencil.

She had prepared her stencils according to the instructions in the section on stencil techniques. She had one motif for the corners and another, with the pattern re-peated twice, for in between. Using sponges and latex paint, she worked as described on page 83. Melanie stenciled in the corners first and then filled in the sides. She estimates that she spent three afternoons working on her stenciled floor.

When the stenciling was complete, Melanie was dissatisfied with the results. Too much paint had crept under the stencil (perhaps this was because the unsealed wood was too porous, or perhaps she had too much paint on her sponge), making many of the edges blotchy and uneven. After the initial feeling of disappointment had left her, Melanie decided to do a little touch-up work. Out came a small paint brush, and soon she was smoothing down some of the roughness. Although it took a little extra time to make the edges neat, Melanie feels that the extra brush strokes made a significant difference in the appearance of the stenciled shapes. Her added touches, combined with the distance between the viewer's eye and the floor itself, help to make up for any imperfection. After all, Melanie was looking at the stenciled floor on her hands and knees. Most people see it from a standing or sitting position.

All of the decorative work had been done with flat latex wall paint, because the unusual colors that Melanie wanted only came in that finish. When the design was complete, however, she gave the floor three coats of satin-finish varnish, which gave it a soft glow.

THE STRAWBERRY DESK CHAIR

For years I sat comfortably in my desk chair, a dark, wooden, junk-store castoff. But no matter how comfortable it was, I could never learn to overlook all of its dents and bruises. I considered it a blight on my studio. In fact, for a person like me, who likes to live with cheerful furniture, it's amazing that I put up with it for so long. But the truth was, I didn't know what to do with it. It was an oak swivel desk chair; the wood was so scarred (even burned in some parts, it seemed) that no amount of paint remover could help. And, as every old furniture buff will tell you, it's a capital offense to paint over oak. There was just so much of that law I could take since the chair was clearly a depressing sight. It couldn't be any worse than it already was, so I decided to decorate it with paint.

I thought a lot about what color I wanted it to be and finally decided on a blue-gray with an antiqued finish. I had never antiqued anything before but I had seen many antiqued pieces in magazines. I searched from paint store to hardware store looking for an antiquing kit with just the right blue-

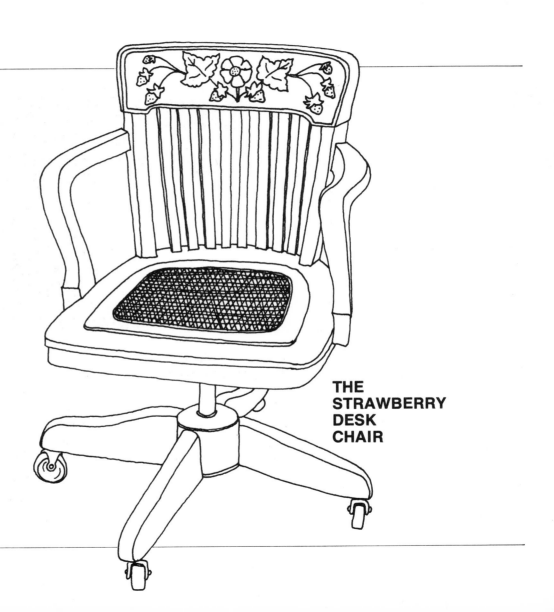

THE STRAWBERRY DESK CHAIR

gray. I was amazed to discover how many companies put out antiquing kits and how expensive they were. The color I wanted kept eluding me, for most of the kit colors were too garish for my taste. Finally I found a store with what appeared to be the right color on the chart, but it was out of stock! In my frustration, I decided to mix the color myself and put together my own antiquing solution. It was a good decision. For information on mixing colors, see page 39. For my recipe for antiquing solution, see page 44.

It took me a long time to mix the color, but I was pleased with it in the end. I sanded down the chair and gave it four coats of paint.

Next, I held a piece of visualizing paper (see page 51) over the backrest (where I intended to put a stencil design) and traced the shape. I found that if I put a desk lamp right behind the chair (with the chair blocking the light bulb), the silhouette of the backrest was very clearly visible on the paper. Once I had the shape of the wooden back, I began to plan the design.

I used an old print of strawberries for reference. Since the design was to be symmetrical, I worked on translucent visualizing paper. When I had completed the first half of the design, I folded the paper over and traced the design through. When I opened it up, I had a complete design. Of course, I wasn't totally satisfied with my first design efforts, but I kept working, and eventually I came up with the final design. This design, on a grid, can be found on page 176.

I darkened the lines of the finished design with a felt-tipped marker for greater visibility and then traced it onto translucent stencil paper. If I had used opaque stencil paper, I would have transferred the design to it with carbon paper. I decided that the stenciling would have to be done in three stages: the strawberries and flower; the leaves; and the flower center. So I actually ended up with three different stencils. The veins on the leaves and pits on the strawberries were painted last by hand.

Using a 2B pencil and pressing firmly, I traced off the design on the stencil paper. I also made sure to mark the front of each

stencil sheet with a big **F** so all the layers would be aligned. I cut the stencil out with a swivel-blade knife.

I taped the first stencil in position on the chair. Although I had done a lot of stenciling before, it had always been on flat surfaces. The backrest of the chair was slightly bowed and this gave me a few moments of worry. What I finally did (and it worked well) was to tape the stencil in position as best I could and then hold each little detail in place with my fingers as I worked.

I applied the paint with small sponges. (Actually, I took a standard kitchen sponge and cut it into three strips.) I dipped about ¼ inch of the tip of the sponge into the paint, wrung it out until it was almost dry, dabbed it on newspaper, and then dabbed it on the stencil. For safety the first layer of paint had to be very thin. This slow procedure was discouraging since I didn't have much to show for my efforts, but only by putting on thin layers of dry paint could I prevent the paint from oozing under the stencil. This was another time when using latex paints really paid off. Water-base paints dry quickly, so soon after I removed the first stencil, the paint was dry enough to begin the second color. The paint did not dry instantaneously, however, so I had to be patient enough not to remove the first stencil or put on the second too soon.

When the stenciling was complete, I drew a light pencil line around the edge of the backrest, freehand, using my little finger to steady the pencil. I used this as a guide to paint in a white stripe. When the paint was thoroughly dry, I erased the pencil line with a soap eraser.

Next, I gave the chair a coat of satin-finish varnish and let it dry for 8 hours. The artwork was complete, but the chair looked "too clean." Now was the time to add antiquing or glaze. I mixed together equal parts of turpentine, linseed oil, and raw umber oil color in a small tin can. Using a stiff brush (and having covered everything in the near vicinity with newspapers) I brushed on this glaze, or "dirt." There was a moment when the chair was totally covered with antiquing that I wondered whether I had made a mistake. With a clean rag I began rubbing away the glaze. I removed most of it, in fact, leaving only the tiniest suggestion of age. It was hard to decide when to stop rubbing. I did know that at all costs I wanted to avoid the overall, even "antiqued finish" that I dislike so much on commercial furniture. But that was easy to do—I just made sure to clean off some areas better than others.

The antiquing, being oil base, took at least 24 hours to dry. It was hard to wait that long to be able to sit in my new chair!

THE SHELL CHAIR

When Al saw my finished Strawberry Chair, he was impressed. He was so impressed, in fact, that he immediately consented to let me decorate his oak desk chair, something which he had previously resisted. As oak office chairs go, Al's was in pretty good shape. When he agreed to let me decorate it, I was delighted (and flattered).

As with the Strawberry Desk Chair, I thought carefully about the color scheme. I finally decided on tan with white trim. I also decided on a symmetrical shell design, which I worked out with shell pictures for reference. The design, on a grid, can be found on page 177. I used all the same methods from the Strawberry Desk Chair for decorating the Shell Chair. This time, however, I was feeling braver about my brush work, so I added some freehand flourishes.

I varnished the decorated chair with a satin finish using an unfamiliar brand that

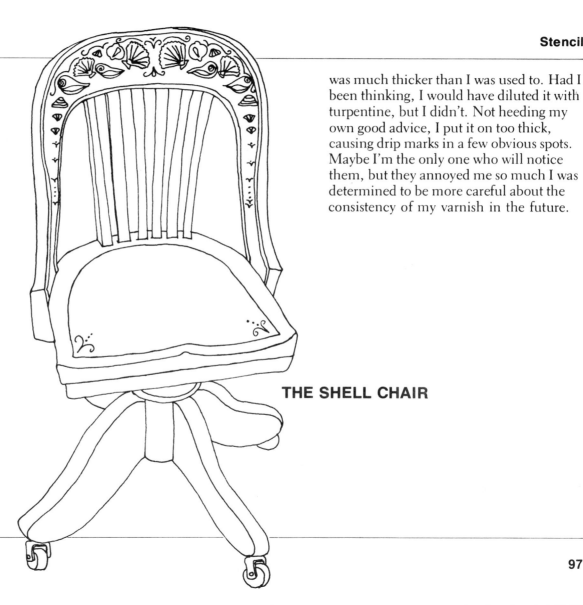

was much thicker than I was used to. Had I been thinking, I would have diluted it with turpentine, but I didn't. Not heeding my own good advice, I put it on too thick, causing drip marks in a few obvious spots. Maybe I'm the only one who will notice them, but they annoyed me so much I was determined to be more careful about the consistency of my varnish in the future.

THE SHELL CHAIR

MATERIALS FOR FOLK ART PAINTING

620 layout pad	medium lead pencil	size 6 round sable brush
acrylic paint	gloss polymer medium	clean water
masking tape	pictures for reference	

16
DECORATIVE PAINTING IN THE FOLK ART STYLE

Decorative painting in the folk art style is the technique of applying a design to a surface with spontaneous brush strokes. Because folk art painting seemed so difficult to me, I resisted it for a long time, but when I finally decided to try, I became obsessed. That may seem a little dramatic, but once I had successfully painted my first cookie tin, I ran around the apartment, and then the neighborhood, looking for more things to decorate. I was used to slow, deliberate techniques like stencil and mosaic and was afraid I wouldn't be able to make those informal, self-confident brush strokes so important to folk art painting. Finally, I decided to take a little of my own good advice. I assembled my materials: artists' visualizing paper number 620; a small, round sable paintbrush, number 6; acrylic paint; polymer medium (all available in art supply stores); medium lead pencil; a jar with clean water; tape; and pictures for reference. For more on the materials, turn to page 35. For a list of suggested references, turn to page 171. In several painless steps, I launched myself into folk art painting, and I'm sure if you are interested that I can help launch you too.

First, here's a rough outline of the steps:

FOLK ART PAINTING-IN-BRIEF

1. Preparing the surface
2. Applying the base paint
3. Transferring the drawing or design
4. Painting the design
5. Glazing or antiquing (optional)

Research

I looked through the books and magazines I had on hand and discovered that there were several easy-looking brush strokes that appeared over and over again. There were also several simple yet charming symmetrical motifs that were good for reference. For more on designing for folk art, be sure to read the section on symmetry that begins on page 11.

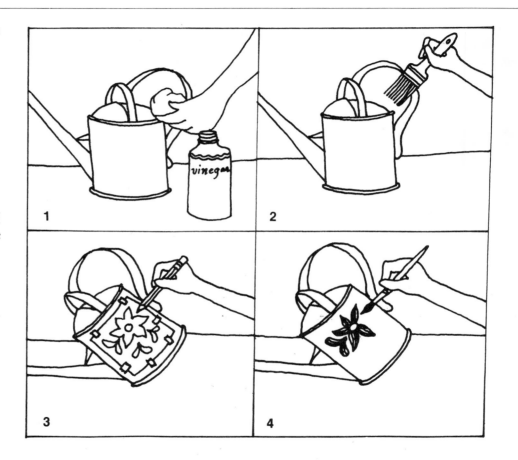

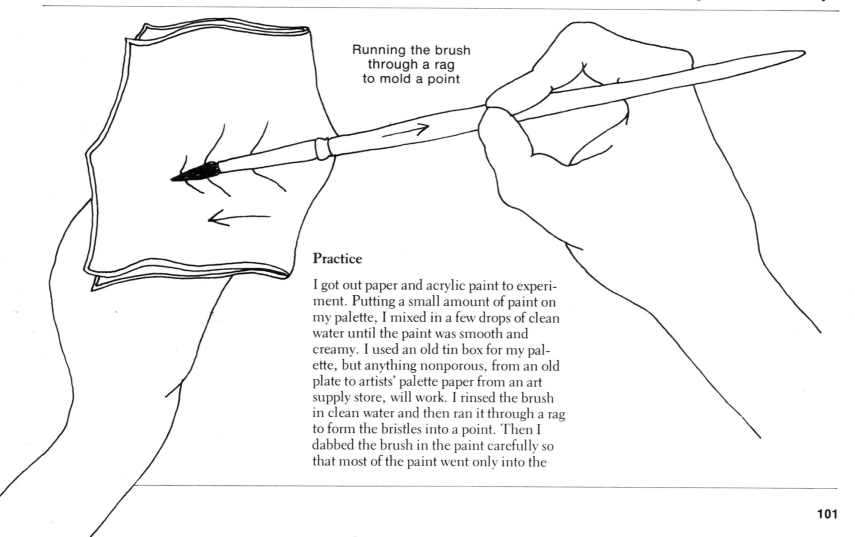

Running the brush
through a rag
to mold a point

Practice

I got out paper and acrylic paint to experiment. Putting a small amount of paint on my palette, I mixed in a few drops of clean water until the paint was smooth and creamy. I used an old tin box for my palette, but anything nonporous, from an old plate to artists' palette paper from an art supply store, will work. I rinsed the brush in clean water and then ran it through a rag to form the bristles into a point. Then I dabbed the brush in the paint carefully so that most of the paint went only into the bristles, not into the metal ferrule above them. I tested the brush and paint on a piece of paper to see how much paint and pressure were necessary to make clear, crisp strokes. Too much paint and the lines were heavy and shapeless. Too little paint and the lines were stringy and broken. If the paint was too thick on the palette, it would stick to the point of the brush when I tried to make marks. If it was too thin, the marks would be watery.

When I was satisfied with the consistency of the paint and the amount on the brush, I began practicing to control the pressure of the strokes. By pressing firmly on the point and slowly lifting up, I made a terrific eyebrow stroke. More pressure and the mark was larger and bolder, less pressure and the line was more delicate. I also practiced long, scalloped lines by moving my brush up and down to make thins and thicks. These scallops are great for border trims. I also made leaves and flowers by grouping together small, repeated eyebrow strokes.

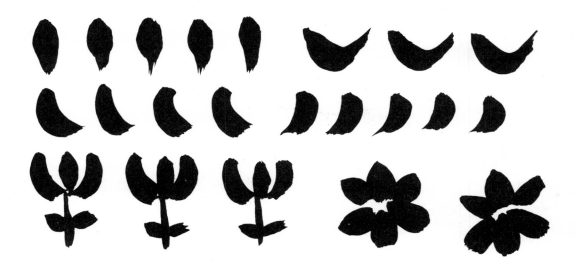

EASY BRUSH STROKES

THE COOKIE TIN

Preparing the Surface to Decorate

I chose a round cookie tin for my first project. After sanding it lightly, I gave it two coats of paint with light-blue latex. Unfortunately, the pattern from underneath was still bleeding through. To remedy this, I coated the tin with high-gloss varnish. (I'm sure this will horrify many experts, but it worked. The bleeding was stopped and there have yet to be any side effects.) When the varnish was thoroughly dry (in 2 to 4 hours), I sanded the tin lightly and gave it a coat of paint. When this coat was dry, the tin was ready to decorate.

To draw a circle I traced around a paint can right onto the cookie tin top. (Cans come in such a variety of sizes that I had to hunt around before I found one that was exactly right.) A compass would have worked equally well. When the circle was drawn, I painted the inside of the circle with tan latex paint. I went around the outline of the circle with the tip of my number six paint brush and then filled in the inside area with a larger, flat brush.

THE COOKIE TIN

Then I traced the outline of the cookie tin top (including the inside circle) onto visualizing paper. Using my reference materials as inspiration, I planned out my design. Actually, I folded the circle in half and worked on half of the design. When I was satisfied with it, I darkened the lines with my pencil. The translucent visualizing paper enabled me to trace the drawing through to the other side. When I opened the drawing up, the design was complete.

SPECIAL NOTE: If you don't have visualizing paper, any other type of translucent paper, such as certain kinds of typing paper, will work. Tracing paper will also work, but I try to avoid it, having found it too flimsy and waxy. With more opaque papers you can still use the fold-in-half method. When you are ready to trace, tape the drawing to a window. The light from outside will enable you to see your drawing. This method, of course, is only useful during the day. A light box is also good for tracing, if you are lucky enough to have one.

DESIGN FOR THE COOKIE TIN

Transferring the Drawing to the Tin

When the design was complete, I traced the lines of the drawing onto the back of the paper using a lead pencil. Do not use a felt-tipped marker. Since I had been using visualizing paper, all I had to do was to turn the paper over and trace. (If your paper is opaque, tape the drawing to a window, wrong side up, and trace.) When the tracing was done, the drawing was on both sides of the paper.

Next I taped the drawing, right side up, in position on the prepared surface of the cookie tin. With a firm hand, I went over the lines again with my pencil. Because I had drawn on the back of the design, the pressure I put on the pencil transferred the carbon lines to the cookie tin. When I had completely traced the drawing, I removed the paper. For information on transferring drawings to a dark surface, turn to page 117.

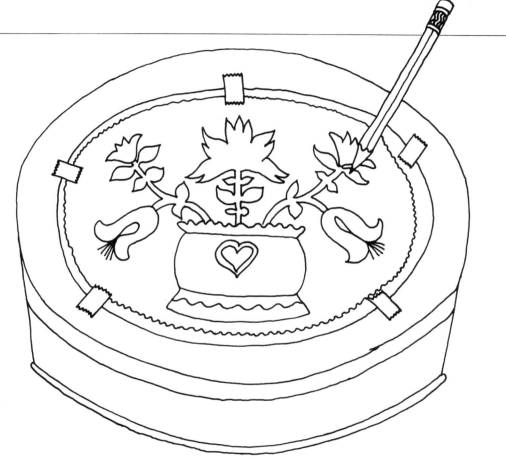

Transferring the drawing to the surface of the cookie tin

Painting the Design

Before I actually touched the top of the cookie tin with decorative brush strokes, I felt it was necessary to warm up. I put a piece of visualizing paper over the original drawing and practiced making strokes. This gave me the confidence I needed to begin painting on the tin.

I actually spent only about 15 minutes decorating the tin, and that included waiting for the paint to dry between strokes. I'm convinced it went smoothly because I was so well prepared. Also, I used only the simplest colors. Besides the base colors of light blue and tan, I used white, red, pink (white mixed with red), three shades of green (two shades direct from the tube and a third mixed from the two other greens), and purple. For more on mixing acrylic colors, turn to page 40.

**PAINTED DESIGN
FOR THE COOKIE TIN**

As I mentioned, after I completed my first cookie tin and realized that it was so quick and easy to do, I went "paint crazy." I turned the apartment upside down looking for things to paint. I decorated my watering can and several baskets (see pages 62 and 67). The next day I searched the neighborhood hardware store, the five-and-ten, and the downtown department store looking for empty cookie tins. I was dismayed to find that there were no empty tins available (although there were plenty with cookies in them). But it was November and the five-and-ten people assured me that they would carry empty tins for Christmas. This experience only reaffirmed my belief that one should never throw out cookie tins. If you have empty cookie tins stashed away in your closet don't be put off by the usually garish decoration on the top. Two or three coats of base paint should cover it completely leaving you with a new, "clean" surface to decorate.

Although my cookie tin search was unsuccessful, I did make some dazzling discoveries. The housewares section of the local department store had a wonderful selection of unpainted wooden accessories including eggcups, spice canisters, and recipe boxes, all perfect for decoration. I also found an exciting line of inexpensive tin baskets, cans, and buckets, all ideal for painting.

The possibilities for folk art painting are endless. Again, I have chosen to decorate what is appropriate to my home and for gifts. I have also been limited in what I chose by time, money, and space. My greatest dream for a future decoration project is to find (preferably on the street, of course) an old armoire ripe for renovation. Naturally, this will have to be in the distant future, when we live in larger quarters. If I found one now, it would have to go on the ceiling.

If you, like me, catch the folk art bug, look around and see what you can find to decorate. Here is a list of objects I have thought of. You can probably add to the list. These same objects, of course, are also great for stencil or découpage decoration.

WHAT TO DECORATE

Accessories

bowls	picture frames
boxes	spice jars
buckets	spice racks
canisters	straw baskets
cheese boards	tins
eggcups	trays
eggs	wastebaskets
flower pots	watering cans
mailboxes	window boxes

Furniture

armoires	chairs	headboards
bathtubs	cribs	hutches
benches	desks	lamps
bookcases	doors	tables
cedar chests	dressers	toy chests
ceilings	floors	walls

Toys

bicycles	rocking horses
dollhouse furniture	sleds
dollhouses	trucks
puzzles	wagons

THE PAINTED WAGON

The Painted Wagon was, for me, a preliminary plunge into painting folk art style. Armed with latex paint and a soft brush, I attacked the wagon with enthusiasm. Unfortunately, my lack of experience in painting on metal got the best of me. A lot of the paint wouldn't stick to the shiny red surface. Instead it kept beading up into tiny dots. I have since learned to wash all metal surfaces down with vinegar and water or lacquer thinner before decorating.

I also worked without a preliminary drawing—I immediately regretted this because I easily became confused. Since then I have learned that careful preparation is a big step toward a successful project. The wagon, when complete, was sealed with spar varnish, which is meant for outdoor use.

Despite my misgivings and my inexperience, I still enjoyed painting the wagon and I am looking forward to correcting my mistakes when I find another wagon to paint.

If, by the way, you have a wagon—or even a bicycle—that isn't shiny and new, you can still decorate it. Sand it, paint it with Rustoleum, and give it a few coats of solid-color paint. It will then be ready to trim. Don't forget to seal any work that will go outdoors with spar varnish.

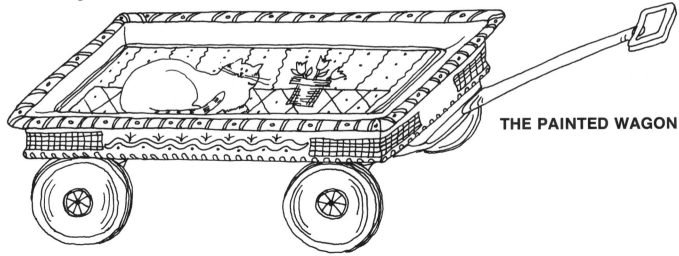

THE PAINTED WAGON

MADAME RATTNER'S BISTRO

When you are invited to dine at the Rattners', besides being sure of a delicious meal, you can also look forward to a few hours in another country. Mme. Rattner has painted her dining room in the style of the inside of a Parisian bistro. The dining table and chairs are decorated with whimsical pictures of food and French inscriptions, while the windows are painted with café curtains, curtain rings, a blackboard for the day's menu. Lettering painted in reverse across the windows proclaims "Restaurant-Bistro." The windows are trimmed with wine bottles and gingham fabric. Just in case there is any question about where you really are, you can see a bustling Parisian street scene, which is painted on a board and hung just beyond the bistro windows. The street scene, Mme. Rattner said, was not in her original plan, but when an addition to the back of the house threatened to destroy her "little bit of Paris," she devised the mural (which is sandwiched between the actual windows of the "bistro" and the new addition to the house) to save her creation. Beyond the windows and the

MADAME RATTNER'S BISTRO

**CHAIR FROM
MADAME RATTNER'S
BISTRO**

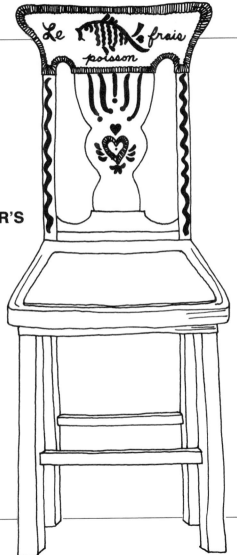

mural is the new bedroom. I wonder what it's like to "sleep behind Paris."

Mme. Rattner did the bulk of the decorative painting in oil-base paint more than thirty years ago, and, although the paint on the table and chairs has cracked, the paint on the windows might have been done yesterday. She seemed distressed at the condition of the table and chairs, but I assured her that for me the texture and color helped to contribute to the overall mood.

Bistro Rattner is a wonderful example of how a little paint combined with a lot of ingenuity can create a room that extends beyond the furniture and the four walls. Even if you are not able to visit Bistro Rattner, perhaps just knowing about it can inspire you to devise your own special painted world.

THE DECO DESK LAMP

I unearthed the Deco Desk Lamp in a stationery supply store. It was a drab, brownish green. When I triumphantly displayed it to Al, he was not impressed. "Oh," he said, "there's been one in my parents' base-

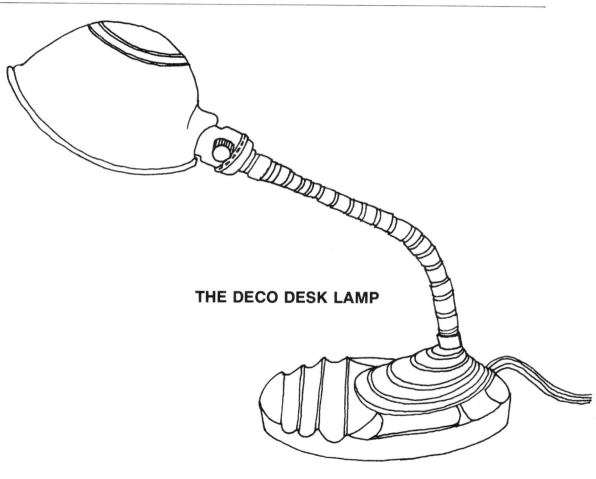

THE DECO DESK LAMP

ment for years." I was crushed. After that I began to see depressing gooseneck office lamps everywhere I turned.

I knew, of course, when I bought the lamp that I was going to paint it. The base of the lamp was metal cast in beautiful, undulating forms. The color was so oppressive, however, that all one could feel when looking at the lamp was unmistakable gloom. Now that I knew this type of lamp was so plentiful, I was even more determined to do a successful redecoration. Think how many people might be inspired to find and redecorate depressing deco desk lamps!

I was able to unscrew the shade from the base of the lamp, which made it easier to work. Using beige latex paint (left over from the Stenciled Shell Chair on page 97), I painted the shade and the base of the lamp. The inside of the shade was a pretty silver color, so I left it as it was. Next I mixed together a small amount of blue artists' acrylic paint and latex white until I had a soft blue. With it, I painted the rim of the shade and some areas on the base. I also mixed pink from acrylic red and latex white, which I used to fill in more of the base and a few lines embossed on the shade. The areas for decoration were so clearly delineated by the forms of the lamp and the shade that I found if I worked slowly, I could fill in all the areas freehand. Using a small, good-quality brush also helped.

When all the paint was thoroughly dry, I gave the lamp a thin, protective coat of satin-finish varnish. My depressing desk lamp was now a deco treat!

PAINTED DOLL DISHES

One rainy Sunday, Al and I visited the Museum of the City of New York at 103 Street and Fifth Avenue in Manhattan. Among the wonderful things we saw there were fantastic dollhouses. The dollhouse builders and decorators had put so much energy and imagination into these miniature homes that everyone who saw them was immediately captivated. The smallest details had been treated with astonishing care. One dollhouse had workshops in the attic. In one room was an art studio complete with canvas, paints, brushes, and paintings. The other room was a woodshop, where the worktable was covered with blueprints, a model of a ship (in progress), and tools—all in miniature.

Later, downstairs in the museum gift shop, I found miniature unpainted wooden doll furniture and accessories for sale. I couldn't resist. I bought a package containing a bowl, two plates, and two mugs.

Using acrylic paint and a tiny, good brush, I painted the dishes freehand. At first I wondered whether this approach was

PAINTED DOLL DISHES

a good idea. What if I made a mistake or didn't like the results? I decided to try anyway. After all, I could always paint over what I had done and start again.

I discovered that the key to decorating miniatures was to work slowly, using simple shapes that were easy to repeat and symmetry (see page 11). What I painted on one side of the plate, I painted on the other. I also let the forms of the dishes guide me (as I did with the Deco Desk Lamp on page 112). The plates had a distinct "rim." This was where I put the flower decoration. The mugs had stripes turned into the wood. I followed these with my paint brush.

I bought miniature fruits on wire in the millinery trimming section of the five-and-ten. I pulled them gently off the wires and placed them on the plates. They were a perfect size. Unfortunately, they were too inviting. One of my cats absconded with several fruits and a mug, which were never seen again.

Unpainted, inexpensive doll furniture is available in museum shops and hobby stores. Poorly painted but charmingly styled Japanese-made furniture is also available. These pieces are worth buying to decorate or redecorate.

You or your children need not have a dollhouse to enjoy painting miniature furniture. Instead, consider setting up little rooms in a shoe box, in a cola crate, or on a shelf. See how inventive you can be.

PAINTED FOLK ART CHEST FOR AL

Because I had liberated Al's first supply chest (see page 21), he soon came home with another. Downstairs neighbors, moving to a new home, had willed it to him. It was a wonderful chest for supplies because all the drawers had wooden dividers in them. Unfortunately, our departing neighbors took with them what must have been a marble top and fancy drawer pulls, because when the supply chest arrived at our door, it looked quite naked.

As with many of our furniture finds, it sat in the apartment for several months being useful but ugly. Al, in the meantime, had found a marble top in his family's basement which was a welcome improvement. But I had plans. . . .

This time I dared not change the nature of the piece because, after all, Al really needed a supply chest. My goal, instead, was to transform an eyesore into an eyeful. If our friends' reactions are any measure (and I hope they are!), then I have succeeded. One visitor wanted to know if the

**PAINTED
FOLK ART
CHEST**

chest was new and couldn't believe that it had been in the same spot for months—undecorated, of course. Another wanted to know if we had bought it in Cepelia (a Polish arts and crafts shop in Manhattan). I was delighted.

The transformation had been quick and pleasurable. One afternoon I gave the chest two coats of latex brown enamel paint. I planned the design on a small drawing of the chest while waiting for the paint to dry. Next I pieced together layout paper with tape and trimmed it so I had paper panels the actual size of the drawer fronts. I worked directly on these. These drawings, on grids, can be found on pages 178 and 179.

Although it took several different sketches, by the time the second coat of paint was thoroughly dry, I had the completed design drawn on two strips of paper. (Two of the three drawers were the same size and shape.) I was ready to transfer the drawings to the drawers.

I couldn't use an ordinary pencil for transferring because it wouldn't show up on brown enamel. So I rubbed the back of the paper panels with white dressmakers' chalk from the five-and-ten. Then I taped the first panel in place, drawing side up, chalk side down (against the wood). I traced over the drawing slowly with a pencil. The pressure from the point transferred a visible white line to the front of the drawers. Later the line was easy to follow with a paint brush and easy to wipe away when the painting was complete.

I had been warming up with small projects (cookie tins, canisters, baskets, and watering cans), so by the time I was ready to paint the supply chest, I was feeling confident.

I worked slowly, mixing polymer gloss medium in with the acrylic paint (see page 39). I also used very simple pastel colors. The painting was finished in about an hour.

Finally, I added white ceramic drawer pulls, which I had carefully chosen at a hardware store because they were of good quality and had an antique feeling.

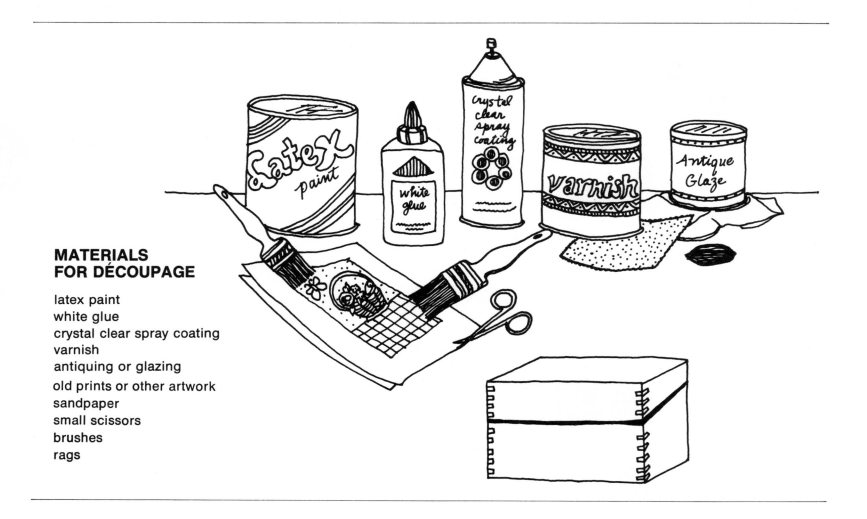

MATERIALS
FOR DÉCOUPAGE

latex paint
white glue
crystal clear spray coating
varnish
antiquing or glazing
old prints or other artwork
sandpaper
small scissors
brushes
rags

The Stenciled Kitchen Floor

The Stenciled Fruit Cabinet
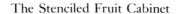

*On the following pages
you will see color photographs of most of the
projects in (Re)Do It Yourself. Browse
through them for visual inspiration and
read about how they were done in the text.
But remember, to use this book successfully, you must also use your imagination.
You may not own the exact chair or cookie
tin that I decorated. The colors I have
chosen may not fit your color scheme. Don't
despair. Instead, adapt the ideas and
techniques presented here to fit your own
needs, tastes, and whims.*

Painted Tins and Cans

Painted Eggcups and Doll Dishes

The Découpage Doll Bed

The Gum-Ball Machine

The Shell Flower Pot

The Shell Mirror

Mosaic Floor Detail and Mosaic Sketches

The Deco Desk Lamp

The Painted Folk Art Chest

The Strawberry Desk Chair

The Shell Chair

17
DÉCOUPAGE

Découpage is an eighteenth-century technique in which the craftsperson cuts pictures from their background, arranges and glues them in place on a hard surface, and then covers the arrangement with many coats of lacquer. Inspired by Oriental lacquered furniture, the French devised their art of découpage. The term découpage comes from the word *découper*, which means to cut out or cut up. Today, découpage is very popular.

I had always admired examples of découpage, and for some reason, I had it in my mind that it was a very technical and difficult craft. Naturally, I was a little hesitant to try it. But in the course of my craft adventures, I decided to do a little research to find out what découpage was all about. As I discovered, there are numerous books on the subject. After browsing through the library and several bookshops, I invested in Leslie Linsley's book *Découpage* (Doubleday). Her enthusiasm, know-how, and common sense helped me overcome many of my misconceptions about découpage. I enjoy découpage so much that even now, as I am writing, I am thinking about my

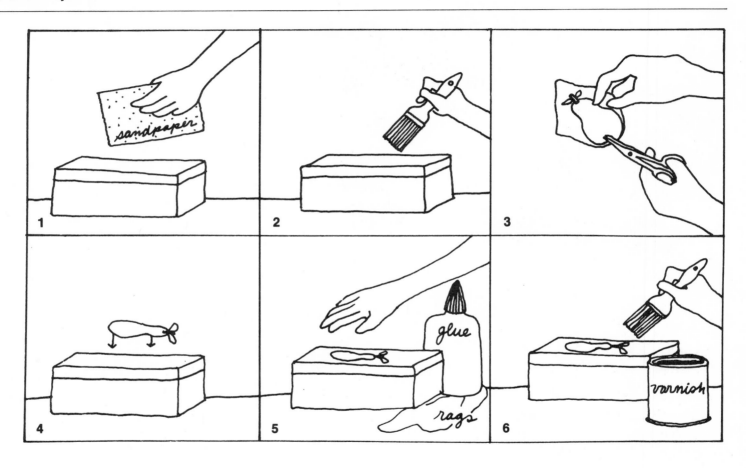

next découpage project. If you too have been fascinated but wary, here are some things you should know.

DÉCOUPAGE-IN-BRIEF

1. Preparing the surface
2. Applying base paint
3. Cutting the artwork
4. Arranging the artwork
5. Gluing the artwork
6. Applying the varnish (5–25 coats)
7. Antiquing or glazing (optional)

First, here is an outline of the découpage process so you know what I'm talking about. For more information and step-by-step details, turn to the Découpage Table on page 128.

Choose a Small, Simple Object to Découpage

Prepare it to receive the artwork by sanding and then painting it. Most objects require three or four coats of paint, but with a primer coat of liquid gesso (see page 27), sometimes fewer coats are necessary. After the second or third coat of paint you will begin to see why it's good to choose a small, simple object to decorate.

Choose Artwork to Decorate Your Object

Look in old print shops, bookstores, craft shops, or museum shops for suitable pictures, or use something you already own. For a first project, choose something with a minimum of details to be cut. Seal all artwork with Krylon Crystal Clear Spray fixative before doing any cutting. If the print has been hand colored (and most have been), this will prevent the paint from smearing when you apply the varnish.

Cut Out the Artwork

Using good, sharp, small scissors, carefully cut the artwork from the background.

Place the Artwork in Position

Experiment with the placement of the cutouts on the piece to be decorated. When you are satisfied with the arrangement, affix the artwork to the surface of the object with white glue. Spread the glue with your finger or a soft, clean paint brush. Apply glue to the artwork only and place the artwork in position one piece at a time, tamping out any air pockets with the side of your hand, your palm, or your fingers. To avoid spreading around unwanted glue or disturbing the artwork, always cover your hand with a clean cloth. Wipe away any excess glue with a moist cloth or sponge.

Begin to Varnish

When the glue is thoroughly dry, in about half an hour, apply the first coat of varnish. Satin-finish varnish is best. (See page 44 for how to choose the proper varnish.) Let this dry thoroughly (overnight) and then varnish again.

Continue to Varnish

When the second coat is completely dry, sand very lightly with wet-or-dry sandpaper (available in hardware stores). This sandpaper, when moistened on the back, becomes very pliable, making it perfect for smoothing over the subtle ridges of découpage. Varnish again and let dry. Continue with the sanding-varnishing-and-letting-dry process until you have built up ten or more layers of varnish. The varnish should cover the artwork and the base object with a clear, hard surface.

If you are using quick-dry découpage varnish, follow the drying schedule on the label.

Antiquing

When you have put on the final coat of varnish and it has dried, don't sand. Instead, paint on antiquing as described on page 45, and rub off with a soft cloth.

Final Touches

When the antiquing or final layer of varnish is thoroughly dry, rub the finished object with fine steel wool and then buff with wax.

Organize

In order to be successful at découpage, it is imperative to organize your materials before you start to work. It is also important to be able to set up your project in an undisturbed, dust-free, well-ventilated corner.

Be Patient

Of all the decorative crafts in this book, découpage requires the most patience. You need patience when searching for materials, you need patience when cutting and gluing the artwork, and you need a vast amount of patience while waiting for the layers of varnish to dry. Although I have been experimenting with a quick-dry varnish (described on page 44), slow-drying varnish is still best.

Selecting an Object to Découpage

Begin by choosing a simple object made of wood or metal. Choose something substantial, something worthy of the thought and effort. I chose a small tabletop for my first découpage project, although every book and article I looked at recommended decorating a small wooden box. A flat tabletop, I reasoned, would be easier to deal with than a box with many surfaces. I was pleased with my choice, although I have gone on to do small boxes.

Preparing the Surface

Whatever object you choose to decorate, clean the surface by sanding. If you are working with an unpainted box or container meant for découpage or other decoration (available in craft shops), all it will need is a light sanding with fine sandpaper. Older pieces covered with their original varnish or paint usually need to be sponged with soap and water, sanded, and then sealed with a coat of liquid gesso (available in art supply stores). Once you buy a container of gesso, consider coating all of your projects with it before painting. It dries in about 20 minutes and sometimes saves on the number of coats of paint required. If you have chosen a piece to découpage that is really caked with paint or varnish, you will have to strip it clean before you can proceed. For more information turn to page 25.

Selecting the Cut-Outs

Selecting the pictures to cut out is the aspect of découpage with the most potential for invention. You will be working with your cut-outs for the next several weeks, so make sure you are happy with your choice. Make sure what you choose and how you arrange it is worthy of being preserved under ten or twenty coats of varnish.

Where to Look—What to Look For

The best place to look for artwork to be used in découpage is an old print shop or used-book store. These places often have pages from cut-up books available at reasonable prices. But be careful: Old prints can be very expensive. Particularly if this is a first project, set a limit on how much you are going to spend. More plentiful prints (that also can be beautiful) are often available for 50 cents or a dollar. Occasionally you will find a reasonably priced old book that is chock full of great material for découpage. If the price is right, buy it. Chances are, the book isn't a rare find, and it's okay to cut it up. (I always worry about inadvertently destroying a priceless book.) If there is any question about the value of the book (perhaps one bought at a garage sale), ask a book dealer before you cut it up. He will either laugh at you or offer you a good price.

Also be sure to choose something you can cut easily. Artwork with tiny lacy details is difficult to cut without practice. Instead choose materials with limited details that need to be cut. The fruit prints I used for the tabletop had a reasonable amount of detail and even they required tremendous patience to cut.

Aside from old prints, there are many reproductions available for découpage. Some of these are excellent, retaining a lot of the charm of the original piece. Others are shoddy, poorly colored, and misprinted. You will have to make the distinctions yourself. Hunt for these better prints in museum shops, bookstores, and craft shops. Check those listed on page 50 and also look through the phone listings for shops and suppliers in your area.

Besides old prints and reproductions, consider old postcards and valentines. There are also more modern possibilities like seed packets, food labels, or your own artwork.

Handling the Artwork

There are several things you should know about the artwork you have chosen.

The paper might be extremely heavy. The only problem with this is that thick artwork requires a tremendous amount of varnish to really cover it. To make the artwork thinner, before you cut it out wet the back with a damp sponge and peel away a layer or two of paper. If the artwork gets extremely wet during this process, dry it between blotters with a heavy book on top to prevent severe curling.

Another possibility is that the paper might be too thin. In this case, whatever is on the back of the artwork will bleed through to the front as soon as you begin gluing or varnishing. The solution is to coat the back of the picture with acrylic

white paint or liquid gesso (again, before cutting out). This will make the front of the picture opaque.

The final pitfall is bleeding artwork. If the print has been hand colored, and many old prints have been, the paint will bleed when the paper is moistened. You may even color a black-and-white print with felt-tipped pens yourself, as I have done, and this will bleed too. Prevent this by coating the front of *all* artwork with Krylon Crystal Clear Spray or some other permanent spray fixative before you begin to cut out the pictures (tiny, cut-out pieces blow around under the force of the spray). If you have any question at all about whether your artwork will bleed—spray. It can't hurt. On my very first découpage project I had this problem. I never even considered that the fruits were hand colored! Now I know better.

Other Materials

Besides the object to be decorated (which has been prepared and is ready to receive the découpage), the artwork, and the fixative, you will also need:

Cuticle Scissors

Good scissors for cutting out artwork are important. Make sure they are sharp because a clean, accurate cut is important. A choppy, ragged cut can only bring disaster.

White Glue

You will need white glue for sticking the cut-outs to the object you are decorating. For standard-weight paper use the glue full strength, but for any paper that is delicate, like paper doilies, thin the glue with a few drops of water. Make sure the water and glue are well blended and apply to the back of the artwork with a small brush or your fingers.

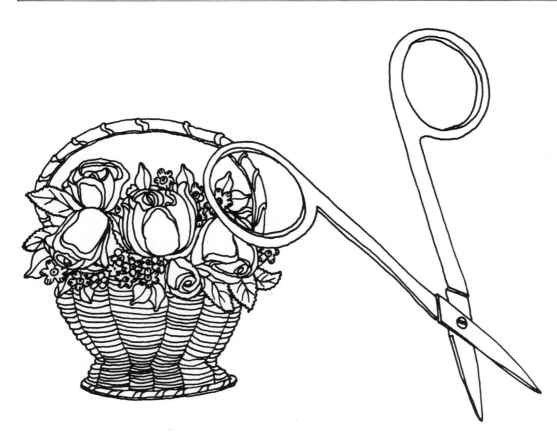

Varnish

Choose satin-finish (my favorite), all-purpose clear, or gloss varnish. Gloss varnish generally dries faster than satin finish. *Do not* use spar varnish, which is meant for outdoor use. It never dries completely.

I recently tried a quick-dry 20-minute varnish developed for découpage. I must admit that I was skeptical. I didn't like the idea of turning a graceful, traditional craft into a quickie project. However, after finishing my first few projects with it, I was impressed. There are certain drawbacks to it, such as the heavy coating it gives, and the odor, which is particularly vile. But if the lure of quick drying time attracts you, it's worth considering. Somehow, I am not yet ready to count it as a replacement for the traditional, delicate look of varnish even though the standard type takes up to 12 hours to dry between coats and should not be applied on rainy days. Don't forget some special thinner. The varnish is useless without it.

Brushes

Always choose a brush that is appropriate to the size of your project. For varnishing, choose a natural bristle brush that will hold up well in turpentine.

Brush Cleaner

Most people prefer to throw away a brush after each project rather than clean it. How wasteful! I think it's because they don't want to wrestle with sticky turpentine. If you use brush cleaner rather than turpentine to clean your brushes, you will be amazed to see what a painless job it can be. Except in rare cases, you'll never again discard a brush before it is worn out. In fact, you'll probably even begin to buy better brushes (which do a better job).

A Glass Jar

Save an old olive or other tall, wide-mouthed jar and its lid to suspend your brush in turpentine between coats of varnish. Puncture the metal top with a can opener and insert the brush handle. Place the bristles of the brush in the jar, which should be half filled with turpentine. This policy will save you from having to wash out your brush every 12 hours.

Sandpaper

Use fine sandpaper to prepare your object to be decorated and to smooth out brush strokes between coats of paint.

Use very fine wet-or-dry garnet sandpaper between coats of varnish to give each layer enough "tooth" to hold on to the next one. Wet the paper on the back and it will become pliable enough to reach all the tiny ridges of the cut-outs. Garnet paper can be used many times before being discarded. In fact, many fine craftspeople consider that it improves with use!

Rags

Use clean, soft rags for cleaning glue from the artwork and tamping artwork in place.

Small Brayer or the Side of Your Hand

Although a brayer (a small, hard rubber roller) sounds exotic and therefore indispensable, I have found that if I cover the side of my hand, my palm, or my fingers with a clean cloth, I have a wonderful tool for affixing the artwork.

Antique Finish

See page 44 for details.

Finishing Touches

Use fine steel wool and furniture paste wax for rubbing down and buffing your finished piece.

THE DÉCOUPAGE TABLE

The table itself was an impulse purchase. One Friday afternoon, after doing the weekend shopping, I noticed a table on the sidewalk outside of the neighborhood junk shop. Although it was covered with a depressing dark stain, I was intrigued by the decorative trim and the silhouette. The price was right, so I paid for it, piled it on top of the groceries, and wheeled it up the street in my shopping cart.

The first things I did were to sponge the table down with water and ammonia, sand it, and then paint it white. Immediately the table was transformed from a murky junkstore purchase to a lighthearted piece of furniture. I was pleased but not surprised, because I had seen this type of transformation many times (turn to page 28 for Painting with White). Soon I began to think about taking the decoration of the table a few steps further. I decided to try découpage. Although I had never done it before, I had always been fascinated by découpaged items. After much research, I was ready to get started.

Gathering the Materials

The first step was to find pictures for découpage. I went through my file and turned up some fruit lithographs that I loved.

SPECIAL NOTE: This is a good example of how grooming your collection pays off. I had been collecting old prints at my leisure for several months so I had some pictures to choose from, but if I hadn't uncovered something in my file that I was enthusiastic about, I would have continued my search elsewhere. There is absolutely no sense in embarking on a long project (and découpage can take a long time) with pictures that you feel only lukewarm about. It's guaranteed that by the time you are finished, you will have grown to hate them. Instead, learn to consider the gathering of materials an integral part of the creative process. Spend as much time as you need looking for materials that you love. For ideas on where to look for pictures, turn to page 50.

THE DÉCOUPAGE TABLE

Cutting

Carefully I began to cut the printed pictures from their backgrounds using sharp cuticle scissors. I soon realized that accurate cutting was a skill in itself, and I was vastly inexperienced. When all the fruits were cut out, my thumbs were numb and I felt that I had a lot to learn. I have been told that cutting becomes eaiser if you hold the scissors stationary and move the paper through the blades, although I haven't yet tried it.

Arranging

Once the pictures were cut out, I put them on the tabletop, face up, and began to experiment with the placement. I arranged and rearranged them until I was satisfied.

Gluing

Next I began to glue all of the pictures in place, one at a time. I left the fruit cut-outs sitting in position on the tabletop. I picked up one piece and spread white glue very carefully on the back with my fingers, making sure that the piece was completely covered. Then I placed that piece in position on the tabletop and pressed it down with the side of my hand. When I was sure the piece was secure, I put a clean piece of paper over it and burnished it down with the flat side of a bottle cap to ease out any bubbles. I continued in this way until all the pieces were in place. I gave the glue half an hour to dry and then applied the first coat of varnish.

SPECIAL NOTE: During this first gluing experience, I made some easily avoidable mistakes. When I was pressing the drawings in position, I tried to use a moist sponge to wipe away the excess glue. I never considered that the prints I had used could have been hand colored with water colors, but they were! When I touched them with the sponge, the colors began to run. Of course,

I panicked. The rest of the cleaning was done with a dry cloth. Since that experience, I make sure to coat all découpage artwork with Krylon Crystal Clear fixative before cutting the pictures from the backgrounds. Once the colors were properly sealed, I could resume wiping the glue with the damp sponge.

The Varnish

Up to this point, things moved very quickly. But once the first coat of varnish went down, the process slowed up considerably.

The varnish I used took 8 hours to dry, so I could only apply one coat a day. Since I ended up putting twenty coats on the tabletop, and I didn't varnish on rainy days, it took a month to complete the work. Of course, I worked on other projects during that time. It really wasn't much of a strain to have the table sitting in the corner waiting for each new coat. In addition, I set up the brush and turpentine, the varnish and sandpaper right next to the table for convenience. I punctured the metal screwtop of a glass jar and half filled it with turpentine so I could store the brush between coats without having to wash it out. The brush was suspended in the liquid so the bristles wouldn't bend out of shape. Some days, when I opened the can of varnish, a skin had formed over the top. I removed this with a wooden stick and discarded it.

I applied the varnish in thin, even coats. Had it been too thick, I would have thinned it with turpentine as described on page 43. I smoothed the varnish on, making brush strokes that always ran in the same direction. If I was working from left to right, every brush stroke I made was applied from left to right. After each layer was dry, I turned the table so each coat could be put on in a different direction. Once the coat of varnish was down, I dusted the tip of my brush over it to break any tiny air bubbles that had formed.

Each coat took about 8 minutes to apply and 8 hours to dry. After the second coat, when the artwork was reasonably well protected by varnish, I began sanding between coats. The sanding put a little texture into the smooth varnish so each new coat would have something to grip. I used very fine wet-or-dry sandpaper. This paper can be made pliable by moistening the back, which makes it ideal for sanding a raised surface like découpage.

Finishing Touches

By the time the table had twenty coats of varnish, the white background had turned a golden color. The white base of the table looked out of place, so I decided to paint it a soft green.

THE DÉCOUPAGE DOILY BOX

After my first experience with the Découpage Table (page 128), I decided to do a little more experimenting before starting another big project.

I chose a cookie tin, sanded it down, gave it two coats of gesso and two coats of paint. I was careful to sand lightly between each coat of gesso and paint.

For the decoration, I used round paper doilies from the supermarket and old paper stickers from Brandon's Memorabilia (page 50).

For this project, I thought I would experiment with the consistency of the glue because I found it too sticky and hard to handle when I did the Découpage Table. Putting some white glue in a bottle cap, I added a few drops of water to thin it. Next I mixed it thoroughly with my paint brush and brushed it onto the back of a doily. As I smoothed the doily onto the surface of the box, I wondered if it would stick when the glue was dry. Miraculously, it did. Part of the reason was, I think, that the doily paper was so thin. I recommend diluting the glue

THE DÉCOUPAGE DOILY BOX

for use with lightweight paper, but I don't trust thinned glue to hold down heavier paper, so I used the glue full strength on the back of the heavy Memorabilia cutouts. After each addition, I wiped away any excess glue with a dry cloth.

As soon as the glue was dry (about 20 minutes), I began varnishing. I gave the box five coats over the next week and the artwork seemed well covered.

THE DÉCOUPAGE DOLL BED

When I first saw the doll bed, it was on my in-laws' basement floor covered with at least fifteen years of dust and cobwebs. It looked like such a permanent fixture, sitting there in all its mildew, that I put it out of my mind.

A few months ago, at the height of my adventures with decorating, I rediscovered the doll bed. My father-in-law, explaining that he had made it for Betsy, his daughter, was curious to know why I was suddenly interested. After I'd explained a little about my experiences with renovating, we went down to the basement together to extricate the doll bed from the dust. We vacuumed

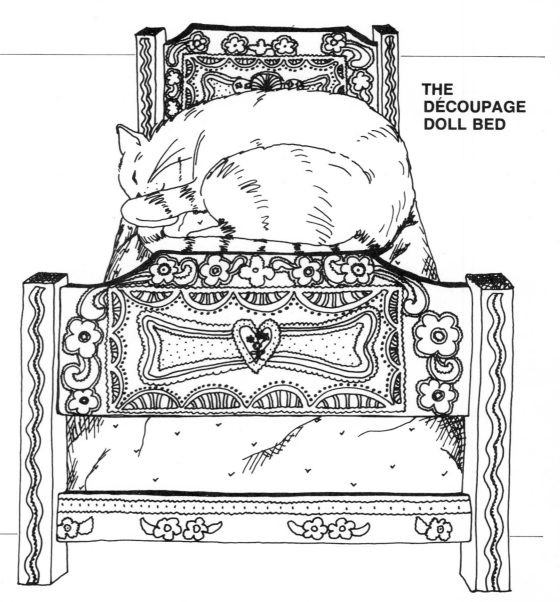

THE DÉCOUPAGE DOLL BED

it thoroughly and then washed it down with mild soap and water. It was a hard evening's work, but when I finally brought the doll bed home, all it needed was a light sanding and a few coats of paint.

I painted it light blue and then began experimenting with the placement of paper doilies that I had bought in Brandon's Memorabilia (page 50). I trimmed down some doilies by cutting off some of the outside borders. Others I cut into individual flowers. When I was satisfied with the arrangement, I cemented each piece down with white glue diluted with about one-third water. I spread the glue on the back of a doily with a soft, flat brush from the art supply store, dropped the piece in position, and tamped it down with the side of my hand. As each piece was affixed, I patted it down with a dry rag to remove any excess glue. I had to be particularly careful not to shift or tear the doilies, which were very fragile when wet.

Once the doilies and glue were dry, I began gluing on flower stickers bought in the five-and-ten. Although the stickers had glue on the back, they were rather thick so I used full-strength white glue just to be sure.

The peacock in the center of the headboard was cut from a firecracker label I had carefully saved from a trip abroad.

When the stickers were glued in place and the glue had dried, I gave the bed two coats of gloss varnish. Later I patched together fabric to make a pillow, mattress, and bedspread.

SPECIAL NOTE: One of the reasons I mentioned the history and the dusty condition of the doll bed is to suggest that you too may find an old piece of furniture or a toy worth decorating in your basement or attic (or the basement or attic of a relative or friend). Once you have caught the spirit of (Re)Do It Yourself, pieces that you have looked at—or looked past—for years will suddenly look different to you. You will find yourself wondering, as I wondered, "Why didn't I do anything about that old doll bed (or chair) before?"

THE DÉCOUPAGE TRINKET BOX

Every book I have ever seen on découpage has a decorated trinket box as one of the suggested projects. When I saw one, unpainted, on the shelf in the découpage supply store (page 50), I knew why they were so popular. The tiny shape and proportions are very appealing.

Although a trinket box ordinarily presents no unusual problems in découpage, I managed to invent one for myself. The lid on my trinket box was slightly raised on top, and I had cut out a circular picture to glue there. The artwork was on stiff paper, and I wondered how I was going to make the picture mold snugly to the lid. I won't enumerate all the wild thoughts I had, for fear of confusing you. The solution, however, turned out to be easier than I had thought. Al suggested that I make cuts with my scissors around the outside edge of the circular picture. I did just that, making sure that each cut was at least as deep as the slanted ridge on the lid. When it came time for gluing, the artwork smoothed neatly into place. The cuts were almost imperceptible.

THE DÉCOUPAGE TRINKET BOX

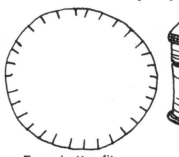

For a better fit on a ridged surface, cut around the outside edge of the artwork.

Side view

MATERIALS
FOR COLLAGE

spray adhesive

white glue

scissors

fabric, ribbons,
    and other trims

Flat surfaces can be covered with fabric to improve their appearance. Although this may not be a "traditional" craft, it is still worth your consideration. Fabric is easy to apply to almost anything—from cookie tins and coffee canisters to dressers and even walls—for a quick decorating project. The possibilities for decorating with fabric are so vast that I haven't even scratched the surface. My few experiments should help you start thinking about some experiments of your own.

There are several ways to affix fabric to a surface—with spray adhesive, white glue, thumbtacks, or a staple gun. With metal objects like the Cookie Tin on page 104, spray adhesive was quick and easy. The decorative trims are held in place with white glue. The fabric base of the Collage Clothes Rack was stretched around a plank of wood and then tacked in place with thumbtacks, although a staple gun would have worked well also. Good objects to improve with fabric include tin cans, notebooks, address books, and boxes. For cover-

18
FABRIC COLLAGE

ing large areas like walls and furniture, try using a staple gun. For more information, look under each specific project that follows.

FABRIC COLLAGE-IN-BRIEF

1. Cut fabric to size.
2. Spray wrong side with adhesive.
3. Mold around container.
4. Apply trimming with white glue.

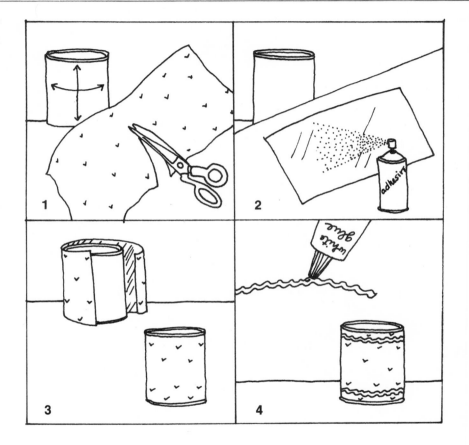

THE FABRIC-COVERED COOKIE TIN

The Fabric-Covered Cookie Tin was one of those projects that was so quick that I wondered why I had never done it before.

Cookie tins, in general, are a challenge to me. They are so useful and so ugly. Recently I resolved that if I was going to have cookie tins around for storing food and household supplies, they were going to be pretty. For ideas on painting cookie tins in the folk art style, see page 104.

I wanted a cookie tin to hold sewing supplies, so I decided to decorate one with fabric. First I covered the base of the tin with a fabric strip cut the exact width of the tin's base, with enough room left to fit comfortably around the outside with a bit of overlap. I coated the back of the fabric with spray glue, and then fixed the fabric in place.

Next I traced the top of the cookie tin on a piece of fabric. To be sure that the fabric would mold to the sides of the top, I made ¼-inch snips with scissors around the perimeter of the fabric. I coated the back of

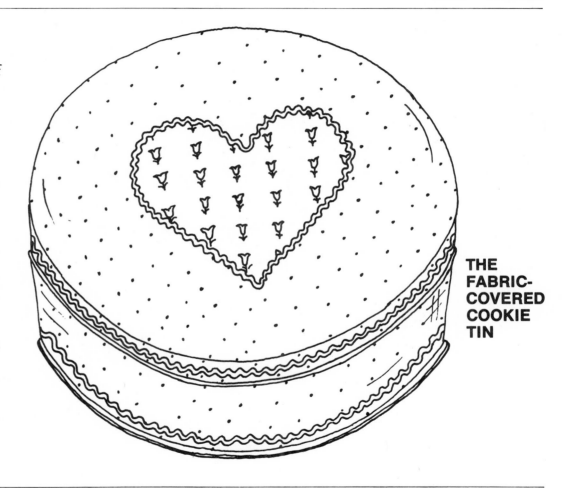

THE FABRIC- COVERED COOKIE TIN

this piece of fabric with spray glue also, and pressed it in place. Because I had cut notches, the fabric molded smoothly around the sides. I pushed out any air bubbles that formed with the side of my hand.

I cut a heart shape from a piece of contrasting fabric and sprayed its back with glue. (For hints on how to draw a heart shape, see page 12.) Then I glued rickrack in place with white glue.

Once the base of the cookie tin was covered with fabric, the top was a little too tight. If you are covering a cookie tin with material and want a better fit, make sure not to cover the entire base with material. Instead, have the fabric end about ½ inch from the top, letting the lip of the tin guide you. For a finished look, paint the uncovered top edge with an appropriate color of paint before applying the fabric.

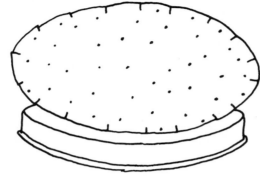

To cover cookie tin top with fabric: trace shape of top on fabric, cut ¼" notches into outside edge, spray back of fabric with adhesive and smooth in place.

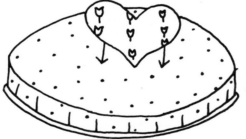

To decorate, cut heart shape from fabric, spray with adhesive, smooth in place. Add rickrack with white glue.

THE FABRIC COLLAGE CLOTHES RACK

The Fabric Collage Clothes Rack is a great solution to the "heap of clothes on the floor" problem. Requiring only the simplest tools and materials, it takes an hour or so to make. When hanging in place, it should catch the eye (and therefore the clothing) of the most forgetful adult or child. Once you've made one for your own home, you may even begin to make them as gifts.

I chose whimsical rabbits in soft colors for my rack because I intended to hang it in my bedroom. You too should choose materials and shapes appropriate to the place the rack will hang. If you are making one for a child's room, choose motifs from a favorite storybook or anything else that might hold the child's interest. If you are making a rack for a more formal area like an entry hall, choose more sophisticated materials like velvet or corduroy. By the way, the whole clothes rack concept can include mosaic, stencil, découpage, or any other decorative technique. What follows is a description of how I made the rack with fabric. My experiences may inspire you to devise your own solution.

THE FABRIC COLLAGE CLOTHES RACK

You will need a piece of soft wood (mine was 7 inches by 25 inches), enough fabric to stretch around all sides of the board to the back, thumbtacks and ceramic hooks (available in hardware stores, five-and-tens, or Oriental import stores). You will also need decorative trims, such as fabric scraps, rickrack, and ribbon, a can of spray adhesive, and white glue. For information on spray adhesive, see page 51.

Iron the fabric and lay it face down on a hard surface. Place the board on the fabric and center it, making sure that the weave of the fabric (and the pattern, if any) runs parallel to the length of the board. When you are satisfied with the positioning, stretch the fabric around one of the long sides of the board and secure it with thumbtacks. If you have trouble pushing the tacks completely into the board, use a hammer. Next gently stretch the fabric on the opposite side around the board and tack. Then do the short sides, folding the corners neatly. Pull firmly as you work so that when you are finished, the front and sides of the board will be covered with a crisp, smooth fabric surface, ready to receive the decorative trims.

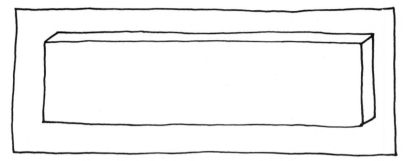

Turn fabric face down. Center board.

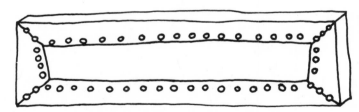

Stretch fabric around board and secure with thumbtacks.

The trims, of course, are totally up to you, but here are some useful thoughts. Plan to put most of the decoration on the upper areas of the fabric-covered base and the ceramic hooks along the bottom edge. This way the decoration will still be visible when clothing is hanging on the rack.

I cut my decorative shapes, rabbits, out of cotton fabric, coated the backs with spray glue, and smoothed them in place. Next I ran white glue around the outside of the rabbit shapes and attached the rickrack. I used small scraps of fabric to cover my fingers as I tamped down the trim because once my fingers got gluey, it became difficult to work. I attached the rabbits' bead eyes with white glue although I used spray glue to attach the ribbon.

I screwed the ceramic hooks in last so they wouldn't get in my way as I worked. Then I added two screw eyes to the back of the rack and strung picture frame wire between them for hanging.

As I mentioned before, the pictorial possibilities are unlimited, so consider whatever you have around the house—buttons, fabric flowers, scraps of denim, old neckties, almost anything.

THE RIBBON MAKEUP BASKET

Melanie Zwerling saved baby-food jars for months because she felt there must be a use for them. One day, to fulfill an assignment in school, Melanie knew what to do.

She lined a shallow, rectangular basket with gingham material by placing the fabric right side up in the basket, tucking under the edges, and applying glue around the top between where the fabric and basket met. Next she trimmed the mouths of fifteen empty baby-food jars by gluing on grosgrain ribbons. Finally she placed the jars in the basket and glued ribbon around the outside edge of the basket. As a finishing touch, she added a bow.

The result is a ribbon, straw, and glass makeup basket worthy of any dressing table. You can use the same principle to make a desk caddy, utensil holder, or organizer for almost any small accessories.

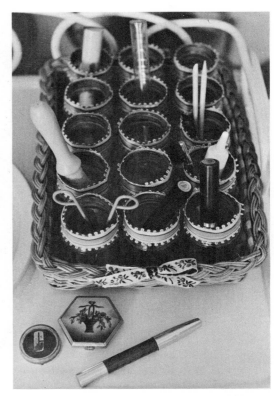

THE RIBBON MAKEUP BASKET

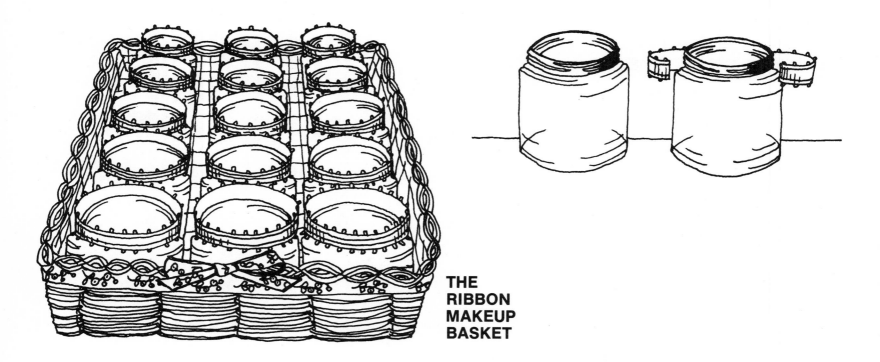

THE RIBBON MAKEUP BASKET

THE SUMMER BAR

The outdoor bar was an early-summer improvement project by Betsy Potter, my sister-in-law, and me. Faced with a weatherbeaten cabinet in need of cosmetics, we wanted our renovation to be quick, inexpensive, and fun to look at.

Betsy suggested using contact paper, an idea I immediately vetoed. Contact paper, as I knew it, was decorated with either garish flower prints or plastic damasks. We discussed the pros and cons a little more, and finally I was persuaded to at least look at what was available. Among the many patterns that we saw in the hardware store were some charming checks, dots, and traditional designs and rich-looking, shiny solid colors. I apologized to Betsy.

Next Betsy and I went home and did a small sketch, keeping in mind the materials we had seen. Estimating the amounts we would need, we returned to the stores to make our purchases. (We had to shop in two hardware stores to find enough prints that were satisfactory.)

At home we used a yardstick and pencil to draw the design right onto the cabinet. Then we cut out the central background pieces and smoothed them in place. Any bubbles that formed were eased out with the sides of our hands. Next we cut out and added the apple, stem, and leaves. Finally (and this took both of us working together), we put on the printed contact paper to border the apple picture and cover the sides of the cabinet.

The finished bar appealed to everyone, and Betsy and I felt that we had met our challenge successfully. We were somewhat curious, however, to see what the life-span of the contact paper would be outdoors. (The label said it was for indoor use only.) Happily, the bar made it through the summer rains with a minimum of damage. It is indoors now for the winter, but come next summer, it will be ready to take its post outside again.

THE SUMMER BAR

THE GUM-BALL MACHINE

When I first saw Betsy Potter's gum-ball machine, I was intrigued. More familiar with the old-fashioned metal kind, I had never seen a modern one made of wood. When I asked Betsy where she got it, she sent me a newspaper ad from California (where she lives), in which a crafts supply store offered these inexpensive unpainted wooden machines. I still haven't seen them available in the New York area, but if they are sold near you, have fun decorating!

Betsy reported that it took her about 15 minutes to add the decorations. First she painted on the flowers and leaves with felt-tipped markers, then she glued on the ribbon, fabric, and rickrack trim with white glue. This is a perfect example of a small investment of time and materials reaping a large harvest of invention and good cheer.

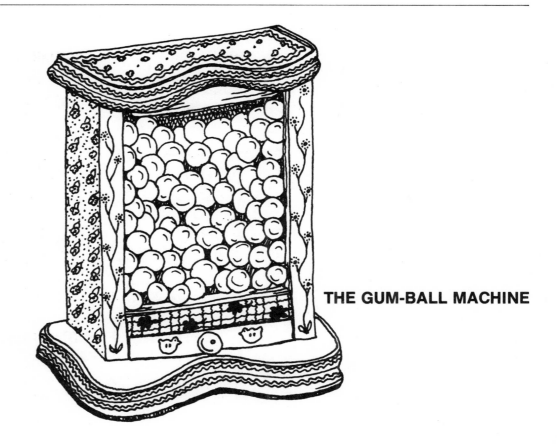

THE GUM-BALL MACHINE

MATERIALS FOR BROKEN-TILE MOSAIC
(INDOOR USE ONLY)

assorted ceramic tiles   tile cutters   felt-tipped marker
tile adhesive   spatula   grout   mixing bucket   squeegee   rags

for outdoors—use mortar instead of adhesive and grout

MOSAIC

A mosaic is created by inlaying pieces of tile, shell, stone, or other decorative elements like beads, buttons, pastas, or grains on a surface. Ancient Greeks, appreciating the beauty and practicality of mosaic, covered their floors with painstakingly arranged pebbles. Throughout history, mosaics done in materials varying from shells to marbles can be found covering interior and exterior surfaces. Mosaic is another of those classical techniques almost lost to us with the rise of mass-produced housing and the alluring efficiency of uniformity.

Early in the spring of 1973, my interest in the possibilities of mosaic as a home craft was suddenly awakened. Driving past the Grant's Tomb community mosaic project on Riverside Drive at West 122 Street in Manhattan, we were drawn by the dazzling colors and undulating forms. Pedro Silva, a sculptor and organizer of the project, had built a concrete armature around the perimeter of the monument. People in the community were invited to decorate the armature with mosaic tile. Those interested were provided with materials and tools, and were given a section to decorate. Although technique and subject matter varied from person to person, the total effect is a visual feast that is exciting and inspiring. As we walked through the giant mosaic, I spoke with some of the people who were working. To my surprise, many said that they had no previous experience with mosaic, and some did not even consider themselves artists! Nonetheless, when I returned several months ago to photograph the finished mosaic, I saw only exquisite work covering the most delightful (and largest) park bench in the world.

Needless to say, conversing with these craftspeople and seeing the results made a terrific impression on me. Soon I had firmly decided that I wanted to mosaic a bathroom floor. I considered covering the bathroom floor in my apartment (which has always been an eyesore), but rejected the idea because I was afraid of laying new tiles over old ones and I didn't want to get involved pulling the old ones up. (I have recently learned that this was an unfounded fear.) Eventually I got my chance when an addition was built on the family beach house. I worked on the floor for several weeks during the summer. It was a satisfying experience that reinforced my feeling that today's bathrooms are uniform and bland not from necessity, but from laziness and ignorance. For more about my experiences with the Broken-Tile Mosaic Floor, turn to page 155.

If you are interested in mosaic but aren't ready to undertake a complete floor, there are many other possibilities. Mosaic tile looks wonderful behind the sink or stove as a splashboard and is easy to clean. But also consider mosaic for a counter or tabletop, as decoration on a box or bottle, or as a wall decoration. Mosaic can be done in an endless variety of materials, but the choice should suit the intended function. Consider pebbles, stones, bricks, shells, marble, polished glass, broken pottery, linoleum, or plastic as well as the traditional ceramic tile.

Here is a rough idea of what is involved in mosaic, followed by a list of what you need.

MOSAIC-IN-BRIEF

1. Choosing a surface
2. Marking the design
3. Cutting the tiles
4. Setting the tiles in adhesive
5. Grouting

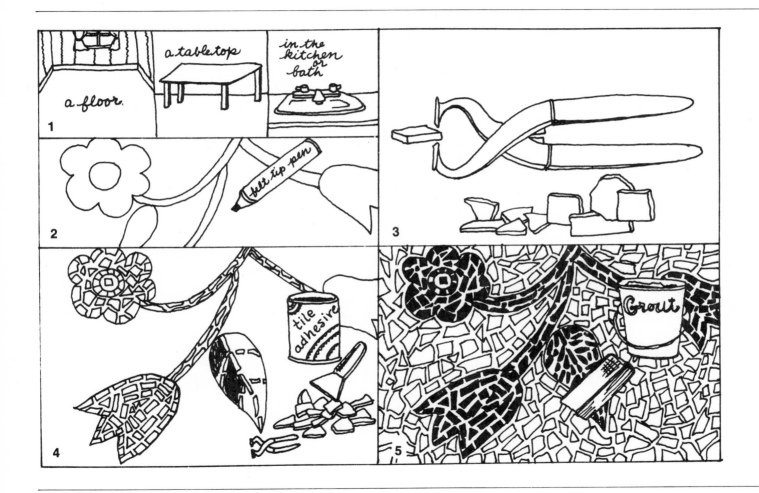

What you will need for mosaic tile decoration:

To Get Started

1. A surface to mosaic
2. Tiles
3. Tile cutters
4. Tile adhesive
5. Trowel (for spreading adhesive in large areas) or old butter knife (for spreading adhesive in small areas)

To Finish

6. Grout
7. Rags
8. A squeegee or cardboard
9. A bucket
10. Water

For shopping information, turn to page 152.

What to Mosaic

Make a mosaic on any clean, dry, rigid surface such as plywood, composition board, thick plastic, glass, metal, ceramic, or masonry.

If you are planning to frame the mosaic and hang it as a picture, or make it into a table by adding legs, be sure to attach these trimmings *before* doing the mosaic work. Protect anything that might stain by temporarily wrapping it in plastic or newspaper or covering it with masking tape.

Preparing the Mosaic Design

Plan your project by first making a rough sketch on paper. Then copy or transfer your plan right onto the surface you intend to cover. For transfer information, turn to page 106. You can also work freehand. In fact, with mosaic, always be prepared to allow the materials to guide you into the unexpected.

Breaking Tiles

For broken-tile mosaics, use tile cutters available from tile suppliers. For the secret to breaking tiles with ease, turn to page 158.

How to Attach the Mosaic

For heavy-duty indoor use, such as on floors, walls, or countertops, tile adhesive works best. It is available by the tube in hardware stores or by the gallon from tile suppliers.

For smaller, decorative work, such as bean, pasta, or bead mosaic, which will not be exposed to moisture, white glue is perfect.

For outdoor mosaic, set pieces into concrete or mortar, available at building supply stores and lumberyards.

Spreading the Tile Adhesive or Mortar

Spread the adhesive or mortar on the surface to be decorated using a trowel or old butter knife (depending on the size of the area). Put down just as much adhesive as you can cover in about 10 minutes (which is how long it takes the adhesive to harden). Then press the tiles into this glue. Any adhesive that dries before you can get tiles in place can be covered with a fresh layer. Work carefully, however, to avoid getting glue on the tiles that are in place. It will take a little experience before you know how much adhesive to put down at a time.

Spreading White Glue

White glue may also be applied directly to the surface to be decorated. Spread it with your fingers or a piece of cardboard. You can also put white glue on the mosaic piece itself (such as a shell or bead) and then drop it in place.

Grout—the Final Step

For indoor tile mosaic, you will also need grout, which is a fine white cement used to fill in the spaces between the mosaic pieces. It is available in powder form by the bag at hardware stores and tile suppliers. Grout is waterproofing, used to prevent moisture from seeping under the tiles. It will not, however, hold mosaic pieces in place, so make sure everything is firmly glued down and thoroughly dry before grouting.

Buying, Mixing, and Preparing the Grout

Buy a pound of grout for every two feet you intend to cover. Mix grout in a clean bowl or bucket (a coffee can is excellent). Put in some dry powder and then add small amounts of water. Stir, using a wooden paint stick, until you have a thoroughly mixed, creamy paste. If your mixture becomes too watery, add more dry grout. Gray powder, available where grout is sold, can be added to tint the grout, although some brands of grout are naturally "off white."

Applying the Grout

Put a large amount of grout on the surface of the mosaic and spread it with your hand, a squeegee, or a square of cardboard. Make sure it falls into all the cracks. When the mosaic surface is covered with grout and the spaces are well filled, remove the extra grout with the squeegee or cardboard. This excess grout can be put back into the mixing bucket. Continue to clean the floor with a damp rag. Keep rubbing and cleaning (change rags when necessary), until the grout is removed from the surface but remains between the cracks.

Work quickly (although it is not necessary to panic) because the grout sets in 10 to 15 minutes. When the grout is completely dry (in several hours), there is usually a thin film left on the surface of the tiles. It can be removed with very fine steel wool or a coarse cloth.

If you want to make the mosaic shine and seal the grout, use silicone polish or liquid wax.

Where to Buy Mosaic Materials

Tiles for floor and wall mosaic are available from suppliers who specialize in tiles. The easiest way to find the supplier nearest you is to check the yellow pages under Tile Suppliers. That's what I did. Tiles, by the way, come in different thicknesses and types. Some are terra-cotta, some ceramic, some glass. Some are meant for floors (the thicker ones), some for walls. Make sure, whatever you choose, that the thickness of all your tiles is consistent.

Lightweight glass tiles are available in hobby shops. But don't eliminate tiles from the tile supplier from your decorative work. They may be a little harder to work with (because of the extra thickness), but the results will be well worth the effort.

Pebbles and stones are available in garden supply stores, hardware stores, and pet shops—or on the beach.

Dried foods—from pastas to ice cream sprinkles—are (of course) available in grocery stores.

Beads, buttons, and sequins are available in sewing supply stores, department stores, and five-and-tens, as well as from mail-order catalogues.

Seashells are available by the piece in shell specialty shops and by the bag in import stores. Also look into shell mail-order firms that advertise in the back of home decorating magazines. For more on shells, see page 162.

All natural objects such as pebbles, shells, and seeds can be gathered from their environment. If you live near water, check out the shoreline. If you eat shellfish (such as clams or mussels) save, clean, and use the shells. If you carve out a pumpkin or grow sunflowers, save and dry the seeds.

UNUSUAL MOSAICS

Mosaic materials may extend beyond the traditional tiles, pebbles, and shells to include materials you can find around the house. Use unusual mosaic materials to cheer up accessories.

You'll be delighted at what you can find for mosaic in the kitchen cupboard. Dry pastas, grains, beans, seeds, candies, and spices, aside from making good eating, make terrific pictorial decorations. The beauties of color, texture, and shape become evident when these little forms are grouped together to cover a surface. Also consider using beads, mirrors, buttons, sequins, or any other small, inexpensive, decorative items.

There are several ways to approach these materials. You can cover a two-dimensional area and make a picture, you can cover the top of a box or table, or you can cover the surface of an entire three-dimensional surface such as an old juice jar. You will be giving new life to a cast-off container.

Draw a rough outline on the area to be covered and then fill in each space with a different texture, or cover a surface with a repeating pattern. Let your pictures be determined by what materials you plan to use, but make sure that everything you use is a dried product and that the base for the mosaic is rigid. If it's not, the mosaic will peel off. Use white glue.

If you are covering a three-dimensional surface such as a can or flower pot, work slowly. Let each area dry thoroughly before turning the object to work on another side. If you want a luster on your finished project, spray it with Krylon Crystal Clear or coat it with varnish. Bottles, cans, and pots make terrific flower or plant containers, but once mosaicked, they should never be immersed in water.

PASTA, GRAIN, AND BEAN MOSAICS

The most fun about working with pastas, grains, and beans is arranging the colors and textures. I love the idea that rice can be dropped randomly into an area of glue, while macaroni can be meticulously arranged in repeating patterns. I also enjoy choosing the materials. With such a variety of pasta shapes and so many types of seeds, grains, beans, and spices, there really is an infinite palette.

The base forms that I used for my projects were an old glass juice jar (found under the kitchen sink), a small wooden truck

PASTA, GRAIN, AND BEAN MOSAICS

- split peas
- lentils
- coffee beans
- elbow macaroni
- brown rice

Wooden toy car covered with pasta and lentils

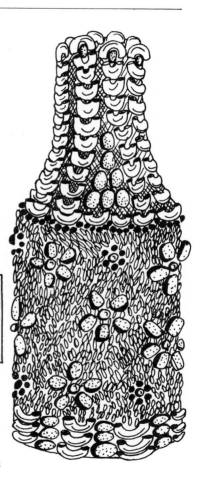

(bought from a natural wood specialty shop), and a plastic flower carton (from our summer petunias). The flower carton, by the way, was a bad choice, because the sides were slightly flexible. I learned my lesson the hard way when much of the carefully placed decoration fell off three days later. Mosaic only on a rigid surface!

The materials I used to decorate the containers included pastas: elbows, bow ties, tubetini, and spaghetti; legumes: lentils and split peas; grains; rice; peppercorns; and coffee beans. I made my choices by what I found around the house or what caught my eye in the grocery store. Perhaps your cupboard will yield a different harvest.

I guided each piece into position with my fingers. Sometimes I spread the surface of the container with white glue and placed the decoration on top, sometimes I put the white glue straight on the material and put the material on the container.

My fingers got very gluey, making it hard to work, so I kept a bowl of water and a cloth nearby for cleaning my fingers. Tweezers or toothpicks might have helped to position the decorations.

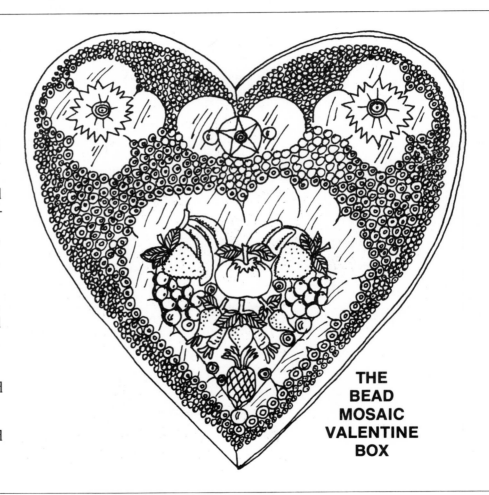

THE BEAD MOSAIC VALENTINE BOX

THE BEAD MOSAIC VALENTINE BOX

The Bead Mosaic Valentine Box was inspired by a delightful gift from my cousins. Knowing my fascination with buttons and trimmings, they collected an assortment from their local button store. I was so captivated by the collection when it arrived in the mail that I spread it out on my desk and started to work.

I decided to decorate a heart-shaped candy box that I had been saving. After first arranging the central fruit motif, I worked outward. The shape of the box and the size of the materials were the ultimate influence on the design. The decorations I used were plastic fruit trims, sequins, glass beads (small and medium), and a few plastic pearls.

I began by using airplane glue because it was handy, but I soon noticed that the glue, when dry, wasn't sticking to the metallic paper box. As a result the beads were falling off. I changed over to white glue (which is more pleasant to use anyway), and the glue problem was solved. I applied the glue directly to the larger pieces and then put them in place with my fingers. For the smaller pieces, like the tiny beads, I filled in the area with glue, carefully dropped the beads in, and patted them in place.

THE BROKEN-TILE MOSAIC FLOOR

As I mentioned in the introduction to this section, it took me a while to locate a floor to mosaic, but after several months, my quest met with success. Next I had to gather materials. Looking in the phone book under Tile Suppliers, I found several listed in my area. I called a few to see if they would be willing to sell me end lots (imperfect sheets). They were.

In order to buy the tiles, I had to estimate approximately how many I would need for the project. Since I wanted to make the pattern and color decisions as I worked, I could only roughly guess the amount. The floor measured 5 by 7 feet, but the shower stall and the toilet also rested within this area. I decided I would need nearly 35 square feet of assorted tiles. Half of them would be white or near white for the background area, and the other half assorted colors for the design.

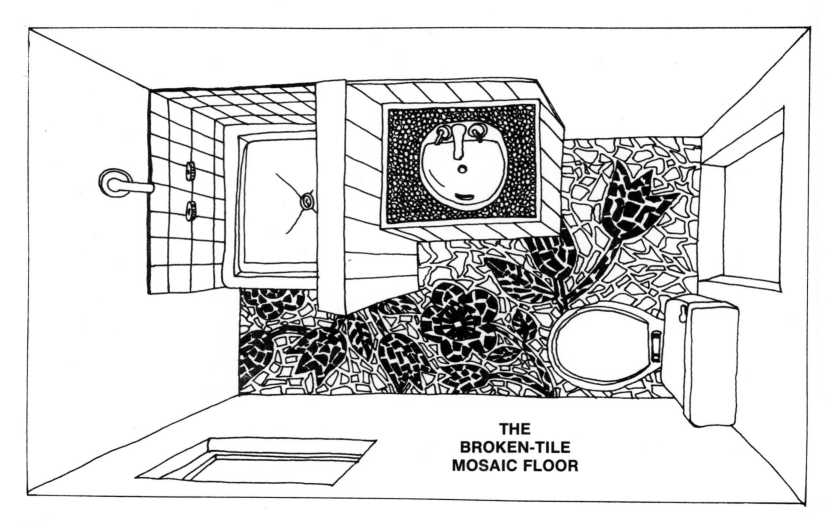

**THE
BROKEN-TILE
MOSAIC FLOOR**

156

This method (or lack of it) may seem a little haphazard to you—and it was. However, it had one significant advantage: cost. Because I was buying a random selection of colors, the supplier sold me end lots that were otherwise unsalable. Because I was taking these tiles "off his hands," he gave me a terrific price.

I also bought a gallon of tile adhesive, tile cutters, and grout from the tile supplier.

Floor tiles, by the way, come in sheets already arranged in geometric patterns glued to nylon mesh or paper backings. Ignore the temptation to lay them down this way. You really can do much better. Instead, remove the paper by soaking the tiles in water (the tiles are often wrong side out on the paper), or peel or cut the tiles from the mesh. The pieces of tile on mesh that resist your efforts can be put down mesh and all.

Seeing a carton of tiles in random colors, patterns, and textures can be sadly uninspiring. When my brother saw the materials I had bought for the bathroom floor, he was disappointed (he told me later). But as soon as I began to cut the tiles up and lay them down in flower shapes, he saw the immediate transformation.

Before starting on the actual floor, I decided to do a practice piece on a scrap of wood. Later in the summer Claudia, age 8, came to visit and was inspired to do her own mosaic picture. Our results are shown on page 5 of the color insert. I wonder if you can tell the difference. I cut tiles for her as I worked on the mosaic floor. She stuck them in place with white glue.

When my practice piece was done, I was ready to get to work on the floor itself. The tiles were to be laid on a plywood underflooring, so I drew the pattern with a felt-tipped pen right onto the surface. Actually all I did was to block in very rough outlines of tulip and daisy shapes connected by stems and leaves. I drew centers in the daisies and veins in the leaves, but that was the extent of the planned detail.

Next I sorted the tiles into piles by color. I put all the white and near-white tiles away because they would go in last, as the background color.

I worked on the flowers, leaves, and stems one at a time. I gathered enough whole tiles in the right colors for a flower, broke them into small pieces, and set them in the glue.

Using an old butter knife, I spread the area to be covered by mosaic with a generous layer of tile adhesive. Working from the outside edge of the flower form inward, I pressed the tiles into the glue. If I was careful that the outside tiles followed the contour of the drawing on the plywood accurately, the rest of the pieces, which were placed fairly randomly, fell into place. I spaced the tiles about ⅛ inch apart, but it was impossible (and unnecessary) to be completely accurate. I just made sure I was as consistent as possible. Since the adhesive remained tacky and workable for about 15 minutes, I was able to stop and cut extra pieces if necessary.

**Detail from
Broken-Tile
Mosaic Floor**

The size of the broken tiles within the mosaic was, of course, variable. On the average, I broke a small bathroom floor tile into three or four pieces. Some I only broke in half, while others I left whole.

I worked very slowly at first because tile-breaking was more difficult than I had imagined. For a while I would recruit spectators into cutting tiles for me. I had begun to develop blisters, and soon I was wondering whether I had undertaken more than I could handle. Then one day there was a terrific breakthrough. The credit all goes to Al. Until that day, we had been putting the entire tile between the teeth on the tile cutter and then squeezing to break the tile. It took tremendous pressure to cut through the tile. However, on that particular day, Al put only half the tile into the mouth of the cutter. He discovered that it took much less pressure to cut the tile. Next he put just a fraction of the tile into the cutter. With a tiny snip, the tile was cut. It was exhilarating because it meant that the worst technical hurdle had been overcome. Tile-

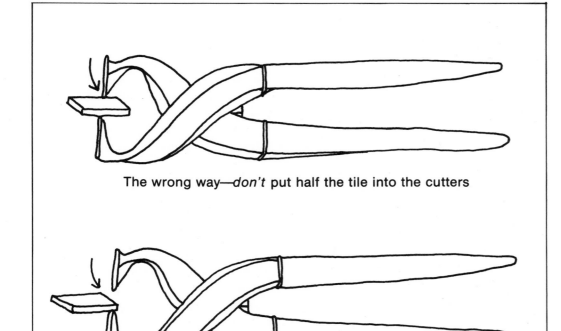

The wrong way—*don't* put half the tile into the cutters

The right way—put *a little* of the tile into the cutters

cutting, from that day on, became so easy that it was fun! The shapes of the pieces are all entirely random, but that is the beauty and surprise of broken-tile mosaic.

Although I carefully followed the drawn flower contours with the broken mosaic tiles, I improvised within the shapes. Particularly with the daisy centers, I enjoyed experimenting with patterns. I found this work technique very satisfying. By following the preplanned flower-and-stem placement, I assured myself of a well-balanced pattern, but by leaving the interior shapes to my momentary whim, I enjoyed tremendous freedom.

When all the flowers, leaves, and stems were complete, I filled in the background. Until this point, my tile color selection had been excellent. But I soon realized that I was badly understocked in whites and would have to buy more.

Once I had the new supply, I broke up all the whites and off-whites and mixed them in a cardboard box. I drew from this box as I worked to assure random placement.

When all the tiles were in place and had been left to dry for 24 hours, Al and I grouted the floor according to the directions on page 151. We grouted twice, however (that's not in the directions). The first time we used pure white grout. With all my enthusiasm for white paint, I assumed white grout would be ideal. I was wrong. When the white grout was in place, the floor looked powdery and washed out. You can imagine my disappointment! But the grout hadn't filled in the holes as well as it should have (we hadn't used enough), so, several days later, we mixed up a batch of gray grout and added it to the floor. It made all the difference. Before the first grouting, I was used to seeing the tiles with shadows between them. The white grout removed those dramatic shadows, but the gray grout put them back.

THE PEBBLE SINK

The Pebble Sink was one of those spur-of-the-moment inspirations. I had worked all summer on the Broken-Tile Mosaic Floor that precedes, never once giving serious consideration to the sink top, which, I knew, would have to be done. In the back of my mind I assumed I would do more mosaic—a perfectly logical idea under the circumstances.

One morning while walking on the beach at low tide, I noticed that the waves had left tiny, smooth pebbles along the shore. For years, watching people collect these pebbles by the bucketful for use in their gardens, I had thought "what a lot of work!" But admittedly the pebbles were beautiful. Each one had a different combination of muted colors and patterns that seemed to light up when wet, and dry to a smooth, subtle surface. Suddenly I began to gather them as if I had never considered it before. "How beautiful they will look sitting in a shallow bowl," I thought.

I brought them home and put them in a small wooden cheese container, where they did look wonderful. I looked at them often that day, feeling the challenge of a lovely material with no immediate use (which, of course, is perfectly all right). Perhaps I knew that there was something more to be done with the pebbles. I went to the beach again, still with no apparent motive, and gathered more.

Several days later, when I was photographing the Mosaic Floor, I reached for the pebbles to fill out the composition. Spreading them out on the unfinished sink cabinet to cover the raw plywood, I suddenly began to consider making them a permanent part of the bathroom.

By the time the sink was installed, I had made up my mind to give it a try. Betsy, my sister-in-law, was visiting from California. Together we gathered more pebbles from the beach, hosed them off, and let them dry in the sun. When they were completely dry, we smeared tile adhesive (it took four tubes) on small areas of the countertop and pressed in the pebbles. Although we carefully lined up the pebbles around the sink and the outer edge of the sink top, the rest of the placement was random. We did,

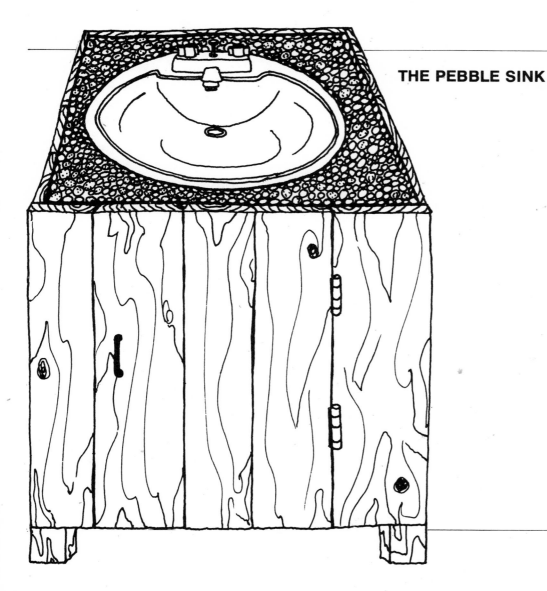

THE PEBBLE SINK

however, eliminate any stones that were too thick to maintain a reasonably level surface. The entire job, with two of us working, took about an hour and a half.

We were very excited when we were done, and the response of those who have seen the sink has been very enthusiastic. Of course, the inevitable question arises of how to balance a drinking glass on the surface. Just to be safe, I think we will use a plastic cup and build a small shelf above the sink. I am also planning to grout between the pebbles.

SHELLS, SHELLING, AND SHELL COLLECTING

Al and I collect seashells whenever we are on a beach. Beachcombing has become one of our favorite activities. We keep our unusual small specimens in a compartmented type case drawer (bought in a junk shop), while larger shells are displayed on tabletops, the mantel, and in glass jars. Still others are packed away in a cardboard carton under the living room couch. When I saw Melanie's Shell Mirror (page 164), I suddenly got inspired to do something with my shells. . . .

If you are interested in doing a shell project but are groaning because you don't live near a beach and never have been shelling—cheer up. Reasonably priced bags of assorted shells are popping up in department stores, Oriental import stores, and hobby shops. There are even mail-order firms listed in the back of home decorating magazines that specialize in shells. Although these ads are generally for higher priced "collectors' items," send for the catalogues. You are sure to find listings for reasonably priced bags of mixed shells.

You can also collect shells (if you enjoy eating shellfish) by shopping in the fish market. Enjoy a delicious mussel, clam, or snail dinner and save the shells. Be sure to wash these shells by boiling them in water with a tablespoon of vinegar. This also applies to shells you pick up on the beach that haven't been thoroughly dried out by the sun and may still contain the animal. Shells that aren't properly cleaned have a horrendous odor.

THE SHELL FLOWER POT

For the base of the Shell Flower Pot, I rescued an old clay pot in which the plant had long since expired. Dumping out the dirt, I washed the pot carefully with warm water and let it dry thoroughly.

In the meantime, I sorted my shells into type and size groups so that when the clay pot was dry, I was ready to decorate. Starting in the center of one of the sides, I applied white glue to the shells and laid them in position, one by one. It was slow work because the sides of the pot were curved and the shells were fairly large. Each time I put a few shells in place, I had to wait for the glue to dry thoroughly before turning the pot or gluing down any shells on top of those that were there. Failure to be patient resulted in calamity! If I moved the pot too soon, many carefully placed shells would slide off. Consequently, it took several days to complete the pot. I worked on a small area, and then walked away to do something else while the glue dried. Another reason it took so long, is that I was determined to cover all of the terra-cotta base. As a result, I had to keep gluing shells upon shells. You can avoid this (as I will do when I begin my next shell pot) by coating the terra-cotta with gesso before applying the shells. Of course, let the gesso dry thoroughly before starting to glue.

I also tried to keep the shell arrangement as symmetrical as possible, hoping to give the pot visual order. But my efforts are nearly lost because no one can see the whole pot at once!

**THE
SHELL
FLOWER
POT**

THE SHELL MIRROR

Everyone who sees Melanie and Michael Zwerling's Shell Mirror is immediately captivated. Its massive frame encrusted with delicate seashells makes a very strong impression. In fact I was so intrigued by it that I wanted to make a shell creation of my own. Because I was afraid that a mirror would be too difficult, I worked on a flower pot. Recently, when I asked the Zwerlings to describe how they made their shell extravaganza, it didn't sound impossible at all, but quite manageable. I do realize, however, that they have put considerable thought into the project, and, in making their first mirror, they were able to solve many problems that might otherwise present themselves.

The inspiration for the mirror came from Melanie's mother, who had been collecting shells for years with the hope of making a shell mirror. Several months ago, when she was ready to begin, she discussed her plans and problems with Melanie. She wanted a shaped frame for her mirror and was having a hard time finding one. Melanie disagreed

THE SHELL MIRROR

with this approach entirely, feeling it would be easier and more desirable to make a simple frame to hold the shells. In the end, Melanie, working with Michael, made her own shell mirror to prove her point. This mirror, shown here, was such a success that the Zwerlings made a second one for Melanie's mother.

If you, like me, are interested in making a shell mirror, here is a list of what you will need and a description of what the Zwerlings did. Although the dimensions for the mirror are given in the diagram, you will have to let the number and size of the shells you have determine the size of your mirror.

1. Three ½-inch by 3½-inch pine strips for the sides and bottom of frame
2. One ½-inch plywood sheet for top of frame
3. A hand saw or power saw (or have pieces cut at the lumberyard)
4. One mirror, ½-inch larger on all sides than the opening of the frame that you will build. Check the phone book for a mirror-cutting store near you to obtain the size you need.
5. One ⅛-inch-thick masonite board 1 inch larger on all sides than the mirror
6. Carpet tacks with large heads in two sizes, one length for affixing the mirror, and another longer length for affixing the masonite
7. Corrugated frame joinings
8. A hammer
9. White paint (or other appropriate color)
10. White glue
11. Shells (For information on where to find them, turn to page 50.)
12. Masking tape
13. Newspapers
14. Picture frame wire
15. Hangers for picture frame

Melanie began by sorting the shells that her mother had given her into groups according to type, size, and color. Then she supplemented the collection with shells from Azuma (page 50), which she bought by the bag. The shells that she bought were shiny and elegant, while the shells collected from the Atlantic shores were weatherbeaten and ordinary. Surprisingly, when the various types were arranged together on the frame, they blended with each other beautifully.

Meanwhile Michael constructed the frame with the wood from the lumberyard.

Although he used an electric saw, the work could easily have been done with a hand saw. You might also consider paying a little extra and having the wood cut at the lumberyard. The sides and the bottom of the frame are made of ½-inch by 3½-inch pine strips. Michael advises that, in choosing wood for a large mirror, care should be taken to avoid using wood that is too heavy. Since the mirror and the shells are going to be heavy, it is best keep the frame reasonably lightweight. The top shape is cut from a large sheet of plywood, the same thickness as the sides. Consistent thickness of all pieces is crucial, warns Michael, having learned the hard way. Because he originally tried to use wood of different thicknesses, the mirror could not lie flat; this resulted in the loss of the mirror (it broke). But the situation was soon remedied.

The side pieces, cut according to the drawing, are held together with corrugated frame joinings. The side with the braces, by the way, is the front of the frame. Shells were glued on top of all these metal pieces, which, Melanie says, helped to strengthen the construction.

When the frame was hammered together, Michael turned it over and placed the mirror (which, as I mentioned, should be ½ inch larger than the frame opening on all sides) over the opening. He then traced the outline of the mirror onto the frame with a pencil. With a ruler, he extended the lines to the corners of the frame as indicated in the drawing. This little trick will be useful later.

When the mirror's outline was marked, he removed the mirror temporarily and hammered in carpet tacks on two sides of the outline as shown. These tacks were not hammered in flush, but instead Michael left enough of the tacks sticking up so the mirror could slide under them and be held in place. These tacks, with large heads, must be at least ¼ inch longer than the thickness of the mirror so enough of the tack can be hammered into the wood frame to provide a good grip. He also made marks on the back of the frame to indicate where picture frame hangers would go later.

Next Michael slid the mirror into position face down and put the tacks into the other two sides of the frame. This, Michael

HOW TO BUILD A MIRROR FRAME TO DECORATE

This becomes the front of the frame. Turn this over to attach the mirror.

The mirror is ½" larger than frame opening all around.

Lay mirror in position and trace the outline. Remove mirror and hammer in carpet tacks on two sides. Slide the mirror in position and insert tacks on remaining sides.

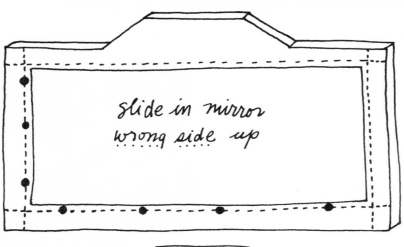

slide in mirror wrong side up

Lay Masonite over mirror and *carefully* attach with carpet tacks. Masonite should be 1″ larger than mirror on all sides.

Turn over to add shells.

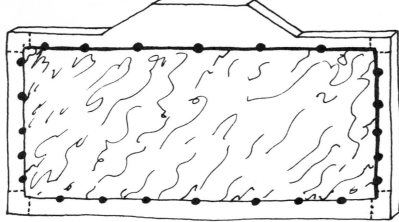

says, can be a little unnerving because one has to hammer very carefully to avoid breaking the mirror.

SPECIAL NOTE: Michael also warns that all work with the mirror and frame should be done on a rigid, hard surface. Any uneven pressure on the mirror could break it.

Finally Michael covered the mirror's back with a sheet of masonite that was 1 inch bigger on all sides than the mirror. However, it was smaller than the outside edge of the frame, so it wouldn't show. He then carefully hammered in the longer carpet tacks through the masonite into the wood frame to hold the mirror in place. Of course, it goes without saying that he did not want to hit the mirror. Since he had extended the outlines of the mirror, he was able to tell where the edge of mirror was.

When the masonite was securely tacked on, without being over-tacked, Michael turned the mirror and frame over so the mirror was face up. It was now ready for Melanie to decorate.

First she masked off the mirror with masking tape and newspaper to protect it from any drips of paint or glue. Then she gave the frame a light coat of white paint. When the paint was thoroughly dry, she was ready to add the shells.

She started by working on the top central crest and devised a striking, symmetrical design. The shells were affixed with large amounts of white glue, which is clear when dry. Then she worked out the corner and bottom designs. When the major areas were complete, she filled in the edges with even rows of small shells.

Melanie worked slowly, over a period of two weeks. When the decoration was complete, Michael carefully slid the mirror to the edge of the worktable. Melanie attached picture frame hangers and wire on the marks that Michael had made while constructing the frame. They had discussed attaching these hangers before Melanie began her shell decorating, but decided it would be inviting disaster, since the mirror would then be sitting on the hangers rather than being flush on the tabletop.

The completed mirror, as expected, was very heavy, so Michael was careful to find the beams in the wall to sink nails into. He advises anyone hanging a heavy shell mirror to do the same or to check the hardware store for other ways of securing the mirror.

THE SHELL HOUSE

I have been fascinated by the Shell House in Ocean Beach, Fire Island, since childhood. Back then, I couldn't understand how a house could be decorated with shells. It had to be magic. Today I realize that it wasn't magic at all, but the work of a very inventive person.

The word-of-mouth research that I did about the house revealed that it had probably been built and decorated in the 1930s, although no one knew the artist's name or whereabouts. The house, today not in the possession of the original owners, is beautifully cared for, and (I would guess) well loved. In fact, beyond the simple façade is an addition that is at least twice as big as the original house. The shell front has been left unchanged except for a clean coat of white paint. The shells themselves have been gracefully sanded and bleached by the persistent sea air.

As I wasn't able to locate the artist, I have no specific information on the materials used to affix the shells, although I assume they were stuck in place with mortar or cement. The shells, I'm sure, were gathered from the shores of the Atlantic, which edges Fire Island.

DETAIL OF SHELL HOUSE

THE SHELL HOUSE

SHELLS

SHELLS

Countless wonderful craft books, reference books, picture books, and magazines are available for craftspeople in libraries and bookstores. The titles listed below are the ones I have found most useful to me for technical information and visual inspiration.

BIBLIOGRAPHY

DÉCOUPAGE

Linsley, Leslie. *Découpage, a New Look at an Old Craft*. Garden City, New York: Doubleday and Co., 1972.

FOLK ART PAINTING

Hundley, Joyce Davies, and Jeanne Davies Cole. *Decorative Painting, Folk Art Style*. Garden City, New York: Doubleday and Co., 1971.

Ritz, Gislind M. *The Art of Painted Furniture*. New York, New York: Van Nostrand Reinhold Co., 1971.

GENERAL INFORMATION ON REFINISHING FURNITURE

Grotz, George. *The Furniture Doctor*. Garden City, New York: Doubleday and Co., 1962.

Johnstone, James B. *Furniture Finishing and Refinishing*. Menlo Park, California: Lane Books, 1969.

GENERAL PICTURE AND REFERENCE BOOKS

Abbott, R. Tucker. *Sea Shells of the World*. New York, New York: The Golden Press, 1962. All the books in the Golden Nature Guide Series are excellent for pictorial reference.

Gillon, E. *Picture Source Book for Collage and Decoupage*. New York, New York: Dover Publications, 1974.

Lipman, Jean. *American Folk Decoration*. New York, New York: Dover Publications, 1972 (a reprint from 1951).

Plath, Iona. *The Decorative Arts of Sweden*. New York, New York: Dover Publications, 1966 (a reprint from 1948).

MAGAZINES

American Home Crafts (American Home Publishing Co., New York, New York). *Ladies' Home Journal Needle and Craft* (Downe Communications, Inc., New York, New York).

MOSAIC

Aller, Doris and Diane Lee. *Mosaics*. Menlo Park, California: Lane Books, 1960.

STENCIL

Day, JoAnne C. *The Complete Book of Stencilcraft*. New York, New York: Simon and Schuster, 1974.

Waring, Janet. *Early American Stencils on Walls and Furniture*. New York, New York: Dover Publications, 1968 (a reprint from 1938).

DRAWINGS FOR REFERENCE

The art work shown on the following pages of grids may be enlarged to any size. Enlargement instructions for this, or any other art work, appear on page 68.

DESIGNS FOR FRUIT CABINET

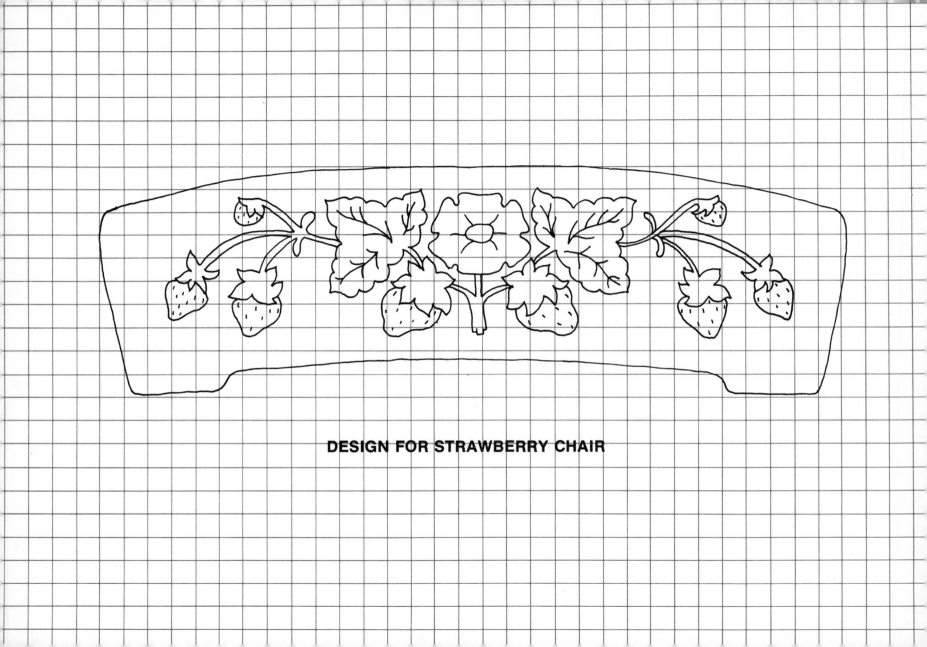

DESIGN FOR STRAWBERRY CHAIR

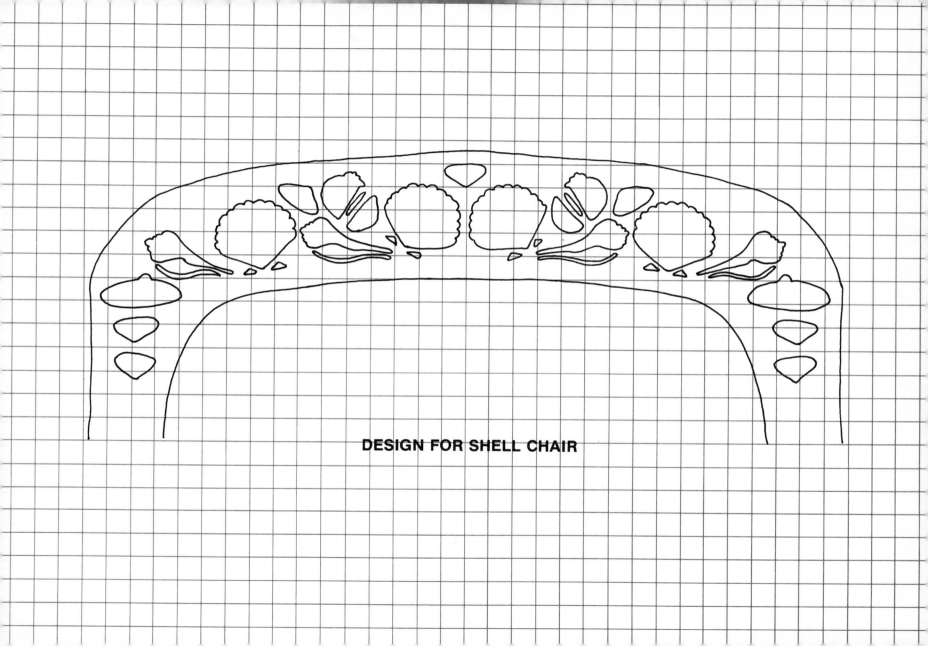

DESIGN FOR SHELL CHAIR

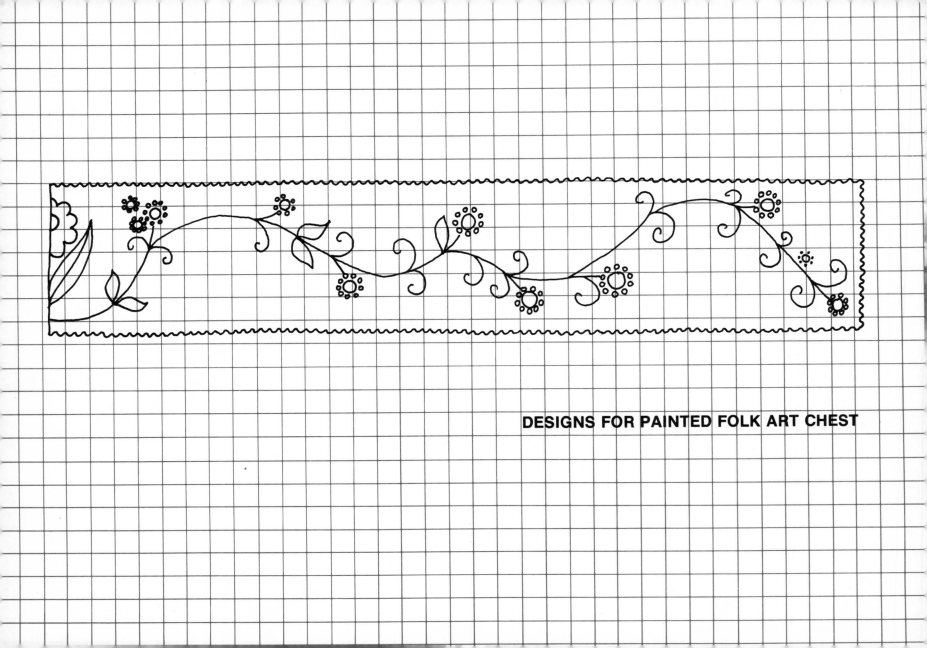

DESIGNS FOR PAINTED FOLK ART CHEST